Imagination and Desire
in the Novels of Henry James

Imagination and Desire in the Novels of
HENRY JAMES

CARREN KASTON

RUTGERS UNIVERSITY PRESS, NEW BRUNSWICK, NEW JERSEY

Frontispiece: *The Woman With a Red Hat,* Jan Vermeer. Courtesy of National Gallery of Art, Washington, D.C., Andrew W. Mellon Collection.

Library of Congress Cataloging in Publication Data
Kaston, Carren, 1946–
Imagination and desire in the novels of Henry James.
Includes bibliographical references and index.
1. James, Henry, 1843–1916—Criticism and interpretation.   I. Title.
PS2124.K34 1984   813'.4   83-23088
ISBN 0-8135-1037-6

To Peter of the leaping spirit

Contents

Preface

The renunciations in the fiction of Henry James are, to me, the most disturbing feature of his imaginative world, as they are also the most persistent source of controversy in criticism of James generally. James's major characters renounce material forms of experience and power for the solitary pleasures of consciousness, vision, and memory. What especially calls attention to the renunciations in James is their element of perversity.

As Sallie Sears pinpoints it, "There is only one necessity in a genuine dilemma . . . the sacrifice of what one hopes is the lesser good for the sake of keeping the greater."[1] In James, renunciation seems perverse because characters who renounce pay twice, losing once by what they give up and a second time through what they keep. Through renunciatory choices, they punish themselves for mistakes, for example, as Isabel and Strether do, and at the same time deny themselves the opportunity ever to undo them. Their renunciations amount to what James in *The Golden Bowl* called "paying with one's life" (24:4). Yet many critics who have reservations about the renunciations in James seem unaware of the extent to which

James's fiction itself promotes their reservations. Such critics have helped to establish and keep in place an unattractive and inadequate stereotype of James as aesthete.

The introduction explores at some length "the house of fiction," the metaphor from the preface to *The Portrait of a Lady* whose ramifications for aesthetic concerns and human relations are the heart of this study. The chapter outlines the established critical perspectives in the context of which I discuss the psychology, aesthetics, and metaphysics of renunciation in James in order to examine his ambivalence toward acts of self-sacrifice. Subsequently, the novels I have grouped together in the chapters work toward their points in tandem. In discussing *The American, Washington Square,* and *The Portrait of a Lady,* I am concerned with the melodramatic loss of self that results from living in parental houses of fiction. *The Spoils of Poynton, The Ambassadors,* and the conceptually transitional *In the Cage* use ambassadorial consciousness as a metaphor for the failures of imagination that result from such a loss of self. *What Maisie Knew* and *The Golden Bowl* show what it means in James to grow out of parental houses of fiction and inhabit structures of the self. Discussion of *The Golden Bowl* falls into three parts: the psychological dimension of the novel, the aesthetic, and the ground that cannot easily be covered by James's achievement in either. The books I have singled out for study and the order, not strictly chronological, in which I discuss them reveal major advances in or clarifications of James's conception of the power of consciousness to find fulfillment in the world.

The jacket and frontispiece show Jan Vermeer's painting "Woman with a Red Hat." Vermeer, like James, was a metaphysician of the (inter)personal, a master of intimate, domestic space. Both proceeded out of a deep affection for the world of ordinary surface detail to portray a reality beyond it.

Acknowledgments

Richard Poirier and Leo Bersani introduced me to James, and their teaching and writing on James and other subjects remain a source of inspiration and pleasure. This is no less true when I depart from their readings. I also want to acknowledge the interest and encouragement given to me in the early stages of this project by Thomas R. Edwards and Alice Crozier. I am grateful to John Carlos Rowe and Henry L. Terrie, Jr., for the challenging readings they gave the manuscript in its late stages.

I feel particularly fortunate to have had Leslie Mitchner as my editor at the press, and Sarah Helyar Smith as my manuscript editor. Washington and Lee University with characteristic generosity gave me Glenn Grants over two summers to help complete the writing and revision of the book. Sidney M. B. Coulling, chairman of the English department at Washington and Lee, showed me untiring support and great personal kindness.

Through Virginia N. Watts and Ken Lane, I first experienced in different ways the most important ideas in this study. It is a pleasure to acknowledge, above all, the friends and colleagues whose largeness of intellect and affectionate regard helped these ideas grow: Theodore G. Albert, Joseph J. Esposito, and especially William McCarthy, whose friendship has steadied and inspired me over many years.

Some material in the chapters "Ambassadorial Consciousness" and "Imagination in *Predominance*" first appeared in journals. I wish to thank *Criticism: A Quarterly for Literature and the Arts* for permission to reprint here, in somewhat different form, "Houses of Fiction in *What Maisie Knew*," (18 [1976]: 27–42); and *ESQ: A Journal of the American Renaissance* for permission to reprint, in altered form, "Emersonian Consciousness and *The Spoils of Poynton*," (26 [1980]: 88–99).

Abbreviations

The following works are cited frequently in the book. Their titles have been abbreviated here for the reader's convenience.

Ralph Waldo Emerson, *The Collected Works of Ralph Waldo Emerson*, vol. 1, *Nature, Addresses, and Lectures*, ed. Robert E. Spiller and Alfred R. Ferguson (Cambridge: Harvard University Press, Belknap Press, 1971). Cited parenthetically in the text as *Nature*.

Alice James, *The Diary of Alice James*, ed. Leon Edel (1934; reprint, New York: Dodd, Mead, 1964). Cited parenthetically in the text as *Diary*.

Henry James, *The Art of the Novel: Critical Prefaces*, ed. Richard P. Blackmur (1934; reprint, New York: Scribner's, 1962). Cited parenthetically in the text as *Prefaces*.

Henry James, *The Novels and Tales of Henry James*, 26 vols. (New York: Scribner's, 1907–1917). Most references to James's fiction in my text are to volume and page number of this New York edition. References to *Washington Square* are to Henry James, *The Bodley Head Henry James,* ed. Leon Edel, vol. 1, *The Europeans, Washington Square* (London: Bodley Head, 1967) and appear parenthetically in the text.

Henry James, *The Notebooks of Henry James,* ed. F. O. Matthiessen and Kenneth B. Murdock (New York: Oxford University Press, 1947). Cited parenthetically in the text as *Notebooks.*

Imagination and Desire
in the Novels of Henry James

–1–
Introduction: Houses of Fiction

HENRY James's central characters generally devote their lives in the end to the solitary and immaterial profit of mind and eye alone. The expense of such vision, to borrow a phrase from Laurence Holland, is nothing less than the renunciation of material experience: those things which for Fleda Vetch in *The Spoils of Poynton* constitute the "spoils" in the largest sense—love, sexuality, sometimes wealth and physical possessions, forms of fulfillment that belong to what we ordinarily think of as the "self." Critics identify the renouncing character of consciousness with the figure of the imaginative artist in James, associating authorial aspiration with material deprivation and loss, and arguing that, for James, art and what is usually thought of as life were incompatible. They seem unaware of the degree to which his novels actively explore his characters' unreadiness to compose the self and profit materially from the design.

Renunciation has become a critical issue in James because the fiction is provocative. It dramatizes a persistent, even when unrealized, effort to imagine a wedding of consciousness with the world of matter. It promotes the sense that James kept extending invitations to his central characters to enjoy material

1

forms of power and profit which they are compromised by their unpreparedness to accept. Naturally it is James who makes them unprepared to accept these spoils, but in fiction as much as in painting, the "negative space" may be as important to an understanding of an artist's attitude toward his material as the "positive space." Negative space, in the context of fiction, refers to the shadow a plot throws, the countershape it projects, or the turn that events in the fiction are responsible for making the reader wish the fiction had taken.

It might be objected that in James, renunciation is not fundamentally regarded as loss. In *The Wings of the Dove*, Milly speculates to Lord Mark about Aunt Maud, " 'She's an idealist . . . and idealists, in the long run, I think, don't feel that they lose' " (19:161). Aside from the error of so identifying Aunt Maud, however, there are problems in setting up this kind of special case for idealists, for James invites us to consider the implicit meaning of idealism, its negative space. Freud connected idealism with repression, maintaining that "the objects to which men give most preference, their ideals, proceed from the same perceptions and experiences as the objects which they most abhor."[1] Idealism may find much of its meaning in what it ostensibly opposes or leaves out of account. It is not a flat concept, but one that throws a shadow, or other self. The proposition that idealists do not feel that they lose is tested by James in contexts that give an affecting sense of presence to loss. Often, it is precisely his characters' inability to feel, to feel loss, that James uses to evoke the reader's dismay.

Renunciation may be regarded as the gesture of both an empathic self, which registers and identifies with the feelings and points of view of other characters, and an evacuated self, which has abandoned its "center" to the fictions or versions of life created in it by the other feelings and points of view that it contains. As Georges Poulet notes in a landmark 1961 essay on James,

With most of the French novelists of the nineteenth century, the central consciousness is . . . the starting point from which are revealed . . . the inner depths of the conscious being. It is quite otherwise with Henry James. If consciousness diffuses itself there, it is almost exclusively outside itself, in zones which are those of external life. James' consciousness . . . turns away from interiority. It is, so to speak, never the center of itself.[2]

This mysteriously decentered centricity or selfless selfhood defines what it means to be a central consciousness in James, and rests at the heart of his ambivalence toward these characters. In decenteredness, James made aesthetic concerns correspond to psychological concerns; he withheld full endorsement from his characters of consciousness because they were failed authors by virtue of being failed imaginers of a self.

The paradox of James's work with the central consciousness, then, is that while it seems to promise a turning inward in which there will be a heightened awareness of the self, it delivers a character aware principally of other selves. Rather than presenting the movements of the inner self, the technique of the central consciousness generally depends upon a withdrawal from personal feeling, sometimes in silence, sometimes in acts of substitution. In these acts of substitution, James's centers either become agents (for instance, ambassadors) for other characters, and assume the burden of emotions that do not derive from them or serve their own interests; or they make other characters their agents and give to them their own feelings. Strether, for example, does both. The result, in either case, is a kind of absence from both the self and the world.

In discussing *The Golden Bowl*, Ruth Bernard Yeazell proposes that "If we prefer Maggie's talk to Charlotte's, it is not that Maggie speaks honestly while Charlotte lies, but that Maggie is ultimately the superior artist—that her language makes for the most harmonious and inclusive design her world can sustain."[3] This, in a sense, is an excellent criterion for mature authorship in James's works. But the only way a design can be made inclusive and lasting, the only way "command of a [given] case or . . . career" can be made what James calls "*supreme*" (*Prefaces*, p. 310), is if the imaginer participates in the design. Tony Tanner, in discussing *In the Cage* as a story of the artist as spectator, concludes with a remark about the heroine which is still characteristic of what is generally said about the figures of imagination in James: "The price she has to pay [for being an artist] is exclusion from participation—indeed it is the very condition of her work."[4] Fleda Vetch cannot protect the spoils at the end of *The Spoils of Poynton*, however, precisely because she promotes a design that entails her own absence. The burning of Poynton is, from one point of view, a sign of her authorial failure, her inability to create "the most harmonious and inclusive design her world can sustain."

The difference between these two ways of relating authorially to the world—the immaterial and the material—is pointed to in a passage from the preface to *The Ambassadors* where James distinguishes between "imagination galore," as he colloquially terms it, and "imagination in *predominance*." Though they may be somewhat imprecise, the terms are suggestive. Speaking of Strether both with pride and a sense of compromise, which reveals his awareness of a challenge only partially met even as late in his career as 1903, James says:

> My poor friend should have accumulated character, certainly
> . . . he would have, and would always have felt he had, imag-
> ination galore. . . . [But] this personage of course, so enriched,
> wouldn't give me, for his type, imagination in *predominance* or
> as his prime faculty. . . . So particular a luxury—some occasion,
> that is, for study of the high gift in *supreme* command of a case
> or of a career—would still doubtless come on the day I should

be ready to pay for it; and till then might, as from far back, remain hung up well in view and just out of reach. The comparative case meanwhile would serve. (*Prefaces*, p. 310)

James proposes in this passage that two kinds of imagination exist in his major characters. There is "imagination galore," the kind that belongs to Strether and to most of James's characters of consciousness, which is evidenced by the failure to take "*supreme* command of a case or of a career." Renouncing the spoils of material experience, these characters surrender the "material" of their lives to other imaginers in the fiction. Possessing the second kind of imagination, "imagination in *predominance*," however, characters may take charge of their lives and make experience their own. Such imagination incurs its costs; by analogy to James, the supremely authorial character has to "pay for it." Yet such characters escape the fate of those who, with only "imagination galore," literally cannot imagine themselves out of the dilemma of paying double: once by renouncing their claim to material power and profit, and again by suffering through a lifetime of alien fictions.

James's famous 1888 artist tale "The Lesson of the Master" offers virtually a parable of the two kinds of imagination. Baldly put, the story concerns a contest for literary fame and love between two artists who exist in relation to each other essentially as father to son. A famous older writer, St. George, instructs the young writer Overt that the only way to avoid the failed and partial artistic achievement of which, he says, his own career provides an example is to renounce love and put aside forever any plans to marry. The "master" concludes the tale by marrying the very woman he knows the younger artist still loves but has renounced on the strength of his advice. Nevertheless, there is nothing to suggest that Overt has become or will become a great artist. Instead, it is the elder writer who, if he writes nothing new after his marriage, has become the supreme imaginer of *this* story, at least. The plot seems to call into question its "overt" lesson about the value of renunciation for art, and to imply that such renunciations are a matter of emotional obedience to characters who function as parents in the text.

Strether has been sent to Paris to perform the ambassadorial mission of bringing home Mrs. Newsome's rebellious son Chad, but he finds Chad so cultivated and improved, and is so stirred and enriched by his own European experience, that he ostensibly abandons his mission; he urges Chad not to return to America. He himself, nevertheless, decides to return to Woollett because he is determined " 'not, out of the whole affair, to have got anything for myself' " (22:326). That is, although he seems to have abandoned his ambassadorial mission, he still thinks like an ambassador, for the refusal to work for one's own profit is an essential aspect of intermediary or ambassadorial employment. As will be suggested later, the imagination in which Strether never entirely stops living, which ultimately presides over his "case or . . . career," is Mrs. Newsome's, since it is she who has defined him as ambassadorial. He refrains from being the author of his situation, from possessing and profiting from the material of his life in a fiction of his own making, because he has renounced its plot to another author.

When James wrote to H. G. Wells that "It is art that *makes* life, makes interest, makes importance,"[5] he was crystallizing his belief that we live in our "compositions" of reality. Art and life both require design, and living is itself an authorial act. This does not mean that life has the perfection attributed to works of art, that it is perfectly ordered or arranged. Living, in James, is an act of authorship because it consists of competing authorial designs: each character tries to possess the material of life in a version of his or her own making. Our lives are our fictions, unless we live a fiction invented by some other author. Mrs. Newsome, whose imagination shapes Strether's life, exists in an essentially maternal relation to the

Woollett editor. For the characters of consciousness, the struggle for imaginative possession of their lives often explicitly coincides with the unfinished psychological business prosaically called "growing up."

James's belief that the design-making processes of life and art are virtually inseparable gives special meaning to the famous metaphor of the house of fiction, which appears in the preface to *The Portrait of a Lady*, and to the language throughout the prefaces that echoes and elaborates on it. "In his addiction to metaphors of houses James had, as it were, an edifice complex,"[6] Robert Stallman jokes. The metaphor of the house invokes parentally authored structures that reveal what it means to be a child, and what it means to grow up. The Freudian conflict between parent and child, authority and independence, formed the basis both of James's fiction and of his theories of fiction-making; it was the prevailing drama of his career. In the prefaces, that drama is embodied in two distinct clusters of images. One of these celebrates structure and architecture, the other celebrates gardens and organic growth.[7]

The *Portrait* preface, where the metaphor of the house of fiction actually appears, offers two pictures of the parent-artist in James's work. In one, the artist is positioned inside the house of fiction, "a figure with a pair of eyes, or at least with a field-glass" (*Prefaces*, p. 46), who watches from the windows of the house. In the preface to *The Golden Bowl*, we find James speaking of his works as his "brood" and his "progeny," and referring to their reappearance in the New York edition, after all his preparation and revision, as "a descent of awkward infants from the nursery to the drawing-room" with the aid of "an anxious needle, the not imperceptible effect of a certain audible splash of soap-and-water" (*Prefaces*, p. 337). In the *Maisie* preface, similar images of discipline and structure appear in response to the defiance, revolt, or intractability of the material, represented by its departure from the house:

"The memory of my own work preserves for me no theme that, at some moment or other of its development . . . hasn't signally refused to remain humble. . . . Once 'out' like a house-dog of a temper above confinement, it defies the mere whistle, it roams, it hunts, it seeks out and 'sees' life; it can be brought back by hand and then only to take its futile thrashing" (*Prefaces*, p. 144).

In the second picture of the parent-artist presented by the *Portrait* preface, he is positioned outside the house and becomes "the soil out of which his subject springs" (*Prefaces*, p. 45). In this very different image of the relationship of the artist to his material, James locates "the germ of my idea" in a metaphoric garden and celebrates instead of chastising its defiance, the "lurking forces of expansion . . . necessities of upspringing in the seed . . . beautiful determinations, on the part of the idea entertained, to grow as tall as possible, to push into the light and the air and thickly flower there" (*Prefaces*, p. 42). In these two groups of metaphors, James implicitly debates how much control the artist should exert over his material, where he should stand in relation to his work and the life on which it depends—in the rooms of the metaphoric house or in its garden. Is it the artist's business to dominate and discipline the material, or should he liberatingly constitute the soil out of which it can grow independently and be independent of him?

James's commitment to the independence of his subject came to him from the two authors he most admired, Turgenev and Balzac. He wrote, in the *Portrait* preface, of Turgenev's regard for the material's own, organic "germinal property": "I recall . . . his reference to the intensity of suggestion that may reside in the stray figure, the unattached character. . . . It gave me higher warrant than I seemed then to have met for just that blest habit of one's own imagination, the trick of investing some conceived or encountered individual, some brace or group of individuals, with the germinal property and authority" (*Prefaces*, p. 44). And in the 1905 lecture "The Lesson of Balzac," roughly contemporaneous with *The Golden Bowl* James rejoiced in "that respect for the liberty of the subject which I should be willing to name as *the* great sign of the painter [that is, the novelist] of the first order." Though Balzac was "intensely aware . . . of all the lengths she [Valérie Marneffe, a character in his *Les Parents Pauvres*] might go to, and paternally, maternally alarmed about them," his parental alarm, according to James, took a benign, uncontrolling form:

> What he liked was absolutely to get into the constituted consciousness, into all the clothes, gloves and whatever else, into the very skin and bones, of the habited, featured, colored, articulated form of life that he desired to present. How do we know given persons . . . unless we know their situation for themselves, unless we see it from their point of vision, that is from their point of pressing consciousness or sensation?[8]

That James's capacity for defining his own authorial relationship to his characters in such purely self-transcendent terms is unstable, however, is evident in the tension between his two pictures of the parent-artist. James felt that for himself as author, as for his characters of consciousness, assertions of mastery over the material were as essential as they were difficult and dangerous.

In the preface to *The Portrait*, the artist at the window of the house of fiction is said to look out on life from "mere dead holes in a dead wall" (*Prefaces*, p. 46), the constraining architecture of his potentially tyrannous relation to his material. Ezra Pound was the first critic to note that assertions of mastery in James are spiked with danger: "The major James . . . [is] the hater of tyranny," of " 'influence,' the impinging of family pressure, the impinging of one personality on another" at the expense of "the peripheries of the individual."[9] A major burden of James's work is the search for a way to divest authorial acts of their sinister quality.

It must be granted that James never fully resolved these difficulties because he saw them as continually regenerating each other. In the dialectic of mastery and submission, tyranny and renunciation, James readily regarded renunciation as the better alternative. Once a character of consciousness, like Maggie Verver in *The Golden Bowl*, had liberated herself from the parentally tyrannical house of fiction, she became the supreme artist of her career, in full possession of its materials. And yet, being so fully in possession, she was then denying other characters—now, in effect, her "germs"—their "germinal property and authority." Thus, what we initially applaud in Maggie as an act of psychological and artistic maturity long in coming for the James character of consciousness ends up as an act of tyranny.

It is of enormous importance, nevertheless, for James's artistic life and our response to it that he finally, in Ralph Touchett's words, satisfied the requirements of his imagination by bringing a character of consciousness to the point of independent fiction-making. In the light of James's desire for "imagination in *predominance*," Maggie's ability to fuse consciousness with material presence and profit provides a standard against which to see James's other major characters implicitly ranged as they retreat from or renounce material experience. If saying this gives a teleological structure to my discussion, it must be noted that James seems to invite such a perspective in implying that his career through *The Ambassadors* may be seen as a preparation for an ultimate development still to come. The pattern of James's movement toward the superlative case from the "comparative case" represented by Strether's imagination (*Prefaces*, p. 310) is doubtless irregular. Between *What Maisie Knew* and *The Golden Bowl*, which I discuss together, and which show consciousness negotiating the world, James wrote *The Ambassadors* and *The Wings of the Dove*, which emphasize the failure of imagination and consciousness to predominate over the material of worldly experience. Despite the achronology of my chapter groupings, however, it is valuable to trace what James himself saw as a pattern of development with a specifiable culmination.[10]

Although James never completely imagined his way out of the tyrannical aspects of the predominating imagination, he tested the boundaries of his fear in depicting a number of collaborative relationships—especially in *The Ambassadors, In the Cage*, and *The Golden Bowl*—in which the dialectic of mastery and subordination is superceded. In collaboration, ideally, equal weight is given to the predominating imagination and its germ; mastery and self-transcendence become outmoded distinctions. In caring to supercede these categories and test the boundaries of his fear of tyrannizing, James set the renunciations in his fiction in a problematic light in one more way.

Leslie Fiedler, whose critical heartiness is refreshing in many ways, sees James as a consummate advocate of the aesthete image of the artist: "The Henry James who began with 'pedestrian gaping' along Broadway . . . is . . . [the same] James who invents the technique of the 'center of consciousness,' i.e., a device for making the peeper the focus of a work of art, and who insists that 'art deals with what we see.' "[11] In a context enriched by references to R. P. Blackmur's famous second introduction to the Dell edition of *The Golden Bowl*, Quentin Anderson compellingly argues that James was inhumanely undisturbed by the strangely fused will-to-power and retreat from experience of his characters of consciousness.[12] In such readings, James emerges as preeminently an aesthete and formalist, rather than as the metaphysician of the social and the interpersonal which I find him to be.

Many other critics of James simply do not find the renunciations or retreats disturbing. Dorothea Krook makes a case for the renunciations in terms of the morally and religiously regenerative power of selflessness.[13] Daniel Schneider's study shows that the current trend in criticism of James is still to argue that the character of consciousness must exert his or her imagination against an imprisoning and debasing material world.[14] Laurence Holland and Leo Bersani defend the renunciations as a necessary and redemptive element of an art that requires sacrifice and loss for the aesthetic profit it finally encompasses, thus adding to the image of James as major aesthete.

Straddling apparent contradictions in a way that is admirably suited to talking about James, a strategy which, quite aside from what they say, in fact may be their greatest gift to other James critics, Holland and Bersani nevertheless contend that the novels are made to absorb back into themselves all of the contradictory energies they create. Both critics allow themselves and James a margin of discomfort with the renunciations—a discomfort that Holland, for instance, registers with such remarkably seasoned qualifications as "the dubious rightness of Strether's folly"[15]—but both writers ultimately show us a James who catches up all such surplus of feeling within the rationale of his fictional system as distilled in the prefaces. Both of these critics read James's novels from the late vantage point of the prefaces with some jeopardy to the fiction. They do this even though, as Bersani acknowledges,

> The novels are . . . a complex critique of the approach to the novels proposed in the Prefaces. The purity of James's structuralist approach to his fiction depends on an indifference to some of the hesitations and conflicts which complicate his characters' efforts to see how living by compositional coherence alone can be made morally workable. The novels are a constantly dramatic struggle *toward* the security of the Prefaces.[16]

Or, to put it another way, the novels stir us, by virtue of some surplus of energy and emotion, beyond what the scientific view of the texts offered by the prefaces can accommodate. The prefaces often distort the fiction they evaluate by sponging it of emotional complexity and moral ambiguity in favor of the relative clarity of propositions about theory and technique. When they turn human complexities into problems of composition alone, the prefaces offer a different version, a different composition, if you will, of the novels' material than the novels themselves provide. One of the issues that is not as calmly resolved in the fiction as it would seem to be in some prefaces is renunciation.

In stressing the importance of compositional considerations over "hesitations and conflicts" in James's fiction, Bersani denies the usefulness of a psychological approach: James's fiction is said to be "notoriously dense in what I suppose we have to call psychological detail, but it is remarkably resistant to an interest in psychological depth."[17] The dangers of psychological criticism are, of course, grave. Much of it distances the text, neutralizing its impact by imposing on it a foreign system or an alien rhetoric, rather than working from within the author's own conception and language, as I try to do by using such phrases of James's as "imagination galore," "imagination in *predominance*," and "house of fiction." The best known psychological study of James, by Saul Rosenzweig, employs a clinical Freudian rhetoric that renders the texts as material for a case study. Rosenzweig writes that the awed sense of inferiority with which the young James regarded his father and older brother William "was solved submissively by a profound repression of aggressiveness" intensified by an adolescent back injury into a "castration anxiety."[18] In his massive biography of James, Leon Edel is sensitive to psychologically significant people and events in James's life and their reappearance in various guises in James's fiction, but we do not always get to see how these have a power and logic that belong to the life of the fiction itself.

Naomi Lebowitz and Ruth Bernard Yeazell, among others, have written important studies that bridge the gap in James criticism between aesthetic concerns and the issues of psychology, character, and desire loosely subsumable under the term "fulfillment." Lebowitz emphasizes the connection in James between artistic composition and human relationships when she writes that James's characters of consciousness become authorial by revising or breaking free of the fixed roles or static portraits assigned to them by other figures in the fiction.[19] Yet for her, renunciation is compatible with mature authorship, while I view it as a sign that the emotional growth which is a precondition for mature authorship has yet to occur, and the character is still caught in a role or portrait assigned by others.

Yeazell bridges aesthetics and human relations by asserting that in the conversations of James's late fiction, characters collaborate, or create significance together. They converse in sentence fragments which enable them mutually to discover, build upon, modify, complete, and expand each other's meanings.[20] That James was indeed deeply interested in the possibilities of coauthorship is suggested by his participation in 1908 in a project of collaborative novel-writing, *The Whole Family: A Novel by Twelve Authors*.[21] Yet collaboratively authored talk is not the highest point of authorial maturity for James's characters of consciousness. Through the reservations with which he surrounds their acts of renunciation, James points beyond collaborative talk to the more elusive ideal of collaboratively lived fictions, versions of experience that people, or characters that represent people, might live out together. Behind the invitations that James offers to his central characters to imagine themselves out of the melodrama of loss and withdrawal is the possibility that fusing consciousness with presence will bring them back into the world to live out, with those they no longer need renounce, reciprocally satisfying compositions of experience. If James never completely realized this conception of human relations in his fiction, he tested it over and over; it haunts his work and gives it its most moving

14

sense of possibility. Failures of imagination of this kind have as much to say about what a writer values as instances of completed imagining.

Such collaboration—shared fictionalizing, or the mutual creation of experience—is the essence of feminism. In its most radical sense, that is, both basic and subversive, I take the women's movement to represent the belief that power can be used communally; that it is better to have power with people than to have power over them; that men and women can collaborate with each other rather than renounce each other or engage in melodramatic rituals of domination and surrender, mastery and victimization. It is surprising, then, to find that most critics of James who regard themselves as feminist are essentially hostile.

One exception is Strother Purdy, a male critic who offers an appreciative outlook on James which is feminist in essence: "To allow . . . that woman is not above us and below, is to leave her just beside us, shorn of the magical powers we know we as men very well lack. . . . To accept woman as one of us [is] to give up her mystification, alternately suppression and exaltation. . . . Henry James is one of those writers who got there ahead of us."[22] More characteristic, however, is the charge that James affirmed the submissiveness, delimitation, and self-sacrifice which typified the condition of women in nineteenth-century society and literature. Judith Fryer, for example, argues that women in James "are not women at all, but . . . reflections of the prevailing images of women in the nineteenth century,"[23] a conclusion that seems to depend on the assumption that a literature which reflects a prevailing condition necessarily endorses it. The result is an analysis of James's fiction which itemizes female stereotypes and overlooks the interrogation to which James subjected the assumptions behind the stereotypes.

Another feminist critic, Nan Bauer Maglin, asserts that James's attitude "towards independent women, the women's movement, and women in general" was "disgust and mockery (perhaps with the exception of women in their 'proper' place)." In discussing *The Bostonians*, Maglin notes that "James's mockery does not fail to fall upon Basil and his marriage to Verena," but she nevertheless maintains that James proposed, in this marriage, to show Verena as " 'rescued' from the supposed double evil of feminism and lesbianism."[24] Yet Verena's rescue by Ransom is as doubtful to James as it is to Maglin. He shows that between the marriage with Ransom and the friendship with Olive, there is little to choose; Verena's idea in either case is to surrender. James's point is that neither choice is viable, regardless of changes in external politics, as long as women's personal psychologies remain committed to patterns of submission.

Judith Fetterley's analysis of *The Bostonians* represents a welcome change in feminist discussion of James: "He invokes heavily conventional assumptions about masculine and feminine nature. But James is not conventional in his assessment of what this material means. He is not dealing in the conventional sophistries of the mystique of feminine fulfillment, the joy which inevitably results from being mastered, dominated, or 'ransomed.' " Fetterley nevertheless concludes that James is guilty of a "more subtle sexism" in romanticizing female suffering, "elevating it to the stature of the tragic."[25] I cannot wholly agree with this evaluation since in his problematical treatment of renunciation, James expends so much energy making the suffering appear supererogatory, willful, or perversely gratifying.

With most feminist discussion of James focused on *The Bostonians*, I want to consider the feminist dimensions of other works by James. It is not my aim, however, to write a strictly feminist account. Rather, I am interested in the critical tool that can be fashioned by redefining feminism, taking it not for female power but, as I have suggested, for collaboratively used or imagined power—a goal that brings us even closer to the established feminist objectives of shared and reciprocal experience. Though it may be the most explicitly feminist of James's works, *The Bostonians* is actually no more concerned with dimensions of experience we call feminist than *Washington Square* and *The Portrait of a Lady*, or, indeed, than any of James's writings that explore the way power is distributed in patterns of tyranny and subordination and, occasionally, is used collaboratively; or which present the costliness of the feminine stereotype that keeps consciousness "in the cage," genteelly separate from the world.

—2—
The Melodrama of Helplessness

Writing on the James family, F. O. Matthiessen hypothesized that Alice James's invalidism produced an elaboration of consciousness not unlike that of her brother's renunciatory characters: "The only world in which she could deploy her force was the inner world of HJ's typical heroines."[1] Although she died specifically of cancer in 1892 at the age of forty-four, Alice James was, for most of her adult life, the victim of an invalidism without discoverable physiological cause. In its effects, her invalidism was like the renunciations of James's principal characters: it deprived her of the spoils of material experience. There is probably no way of knowing the precise role that James's observation of his sister's life in the family played in his conception of the character of consciousness. It would be useful, nevertheless, to explore in some detail Alice James's relationship with the senior Henry James because it provides a clarifying analogue for the relationship of parents and children in James's fiction and the way in which that relationship fosters renunciation.

In a hair-raising diary entry in which she looks back to the time when she was nine or ten, Alice James locates the beginnings of her invalidism in episodes of hysteria in which her anger and defiance, whether held in or released, expressed themselves by rendering her helpless. Whether she imposed on herself the "straitjacket" of self-control, or "abandon[ed]" herself to "upheaval," she found herself immobilized, "abjectly impotent":

As I used to sit immovable reading in the library with waves of violent inclination suddenly invading my muscles taking some one of their varied forms such as throwing myself out of the window, or knocking off the head of the benignant pater as he sat with his silver locks, writing at his table, it used to seem to me that the only difference between me and the insane was that I had not only all the horrors and suffering of insanity but the duties of doctor, nurse, and straitjacket imposed upon me, too. Conceive of never being without the sense that if you let yourself go for a moment your mechanism will fall into a pie and that at some given moment you must abandon it all, let the dykes break and the flood sweep in, acknowledging yourself abjectly impotent before the immutable laws. . . . When the fancy took me of a morning at school to *study* my lessons by way of variety instead of shirking or wiggling thro' the most impossible sensations of upheaval, violent revolt in my head overtook me. . . . Anything that sticks of itself is free to do so, but conscious and continuous cerebration is an impossible exercise. (*Diary*, pp. 149–50)

The peculiar mixture of "violent revolt" and helplessness revealed in this passage is critical.

Juxtaposed to the suicide contemplated—"throwing myself out of the window"—is the fantasized rebellion against her father: "knocking off the head of the benignant pater." The elder James's response to both assertions of self seems to have been a belittling agreeableness. Ruth Bernard Yeazell notes a letter that Henry senior wrote to his youngest son, Robertson, about Alice's continuing interest in suicide, the first form of self-assertion: "I told her that so far as I was concerned she had my full permission to end her life whenever she pleased; only I hoped that if ever she felt like doing that sort of justice to her circumstances, she would do it in a perfectly gentle way in order not to distress her friends." Yeazell comments: "Though Alice's question has posed an obscure challenge, Henry Sr. implicitly refuses to be drawn into battle . . . the lack of paternal resistance . . . drains the threatened gesture of its most potent meaning. By readily acknowledging Alice's right to destroy herself, her father had rendered her powerless to do so." In the dynamics of this relationship, only death can complete the assertion of filial independence: "Suicide clearly tempted her as an absolute act of will: for the thirty-year-old woman, it would also have proved the ultimate means of leaving home."[2] Yet death, like the rebellious invalidism in which she went on living, would have been an act of negative will, a way of saying no, which would have left her, as it leaves Milly in *The Wings of the Dove*, no way to say yes, no way to assert a positive identity.

About her effort to assert herself in the second way, through direct filial rebellion, Alice comments: "I am not rebellious by temperament and have trampled down as much as possible all boresome insurrections, having fortunately early perceived that the figure of abortive rebel lent itself much more to the comic than the heroic in the eye of the cold-blooded observer" (*Diary*, p. 119). Because he views it as an occasion for mirth, "the cold-blooded observer" again robs the rebelliousness which is a natural step toward maturity of any claim to serious attention or respect. In *Washington Square*, Catherine Sloper's "satiric parent" (p. 228) is a "cold-blooded observer" from whom Catherine likewise accepts a belittling jocularity that prevents her from completing her revolt and achieving full independence.

Writing these passages in 1890, some thirty years after the

scenes they describe took place, Alice James apparently no longer felt as "abjectly impotent" as she says she felt in childhood, for she tackles their angry intensity with the sophistication of a highly contrived and depersonalizing literary style. In this style, "conscious and continuous cerebration" has become a possibility, and a great comfort. The father she would have liked to kill is aesthetically distanced as "the benignant pater," complete with benevolent and theatrical "silver locks." She laughs at her anger and hides it in the satirized persona of "abortive rebel," engaged in "boresome insurrections," whose violence is deflected by safely Latinate rhetoric. Hostile emotions are thus protectively discharged as a joke and an occasion for verbal display. The passages suggest defiance, but talk their way around it. For all of their rhetorical sophistication, they reveal an essential silence.

Alice James expressed her feelings indirectly, in self-reflexive irony and psychosomatic invalidism, forms of assertiveness that masquerade as helplessness. In the process, she became helpless. In the guise of invalid, the otherwise "abortive rebel" could command serious attention from "the cold-blooded observer."[3] At the same time, this seeming assertiveness obviously was not successful, as it perpetuated the very dependence that it was intended to reverse—it prevented any real assertion of self from reaching maturity, the actual departure from a parental house of fiction. Her sense of herself remained the one she had received from her father even after his death. Until she died, she lived in this fiction of her helplessness, a psychosomatic invalid or "abortive rebel." Ultimately, then, she was defined by the person she resisted. Indirectly resisting him through irony and invalidism prevented her from getting beyond resistance.

Alice James's only partially delivered rebellion and the resulting paralysis parallel the renunciations of James's characters of consciousness and the art of negation by means of which they most often define themselves. This art of negation has affinities with the concept of negation that Freud saw as a close cousin to repression. Repression is linked to the shadow self, the psyche's negative space relative to the positive space of the conscious mind. Freud proposed that "The content of a repressed image or idea can make its way into consciousness, [only] on condition that it is *negated*. Negation is a way of taking cognizance of [that is, accepting into the conscious mind] what is repressed. . . . The outcome of this is a kind of intellectual acceptance of the repressed, while at the same time what is essential to the repression persists."[4]

Silencing open assertions of rebellion, Catherine Sloper of *Washington Square*, Claire de Cintré of *The American*, Isabel of *The Portrait*, and Strether of *The Ambassadors* all generate a sense of self by negating—or saying no to—other characters, who consequently hold their independence and their imaginations in custody. When James's characters of consciousness resist the fictions of others instead of truly reinventing them, they remain defined by them in a kind of negative counter-image. Thus Milly in *The Wings of the Dove* is still held by Kate and Densher even though she withdraws from them when she discovers their secret. It might even be said that in some sense Milly dies because she believes in Kate and Densher's fiction of her as romantically doomed and close to death. Her bid from beyond the grave to be the supreme imaginer of their situation through the instrumentality of her "will" is bound to fail because her literal and figurative absence from the design she promotes conforms to their vision of life, rather than her own desires.

THE AMERICAN

It is apparent from the three novels on which this chapter focuses that renunciation and childhood, or childhood states, existed in suggestive association in James's mind. *The American*

(1877) is, for the purposes of this study, an especially good place to begin because it distinguishes between two modalities of renunciation and thus makes it easier to isolate the mode that occurs most frequently in James. Newman's renunciation is atypical. The revenge and the obsession with lost love that he gives up do not seem to be great losses, so that his renouncing them does not strike us as an act of overwrought self-transcendence on the order of Strether's determination " 'Not, out of the whole affair, to have got anything for myself ' " (22:326). Claire's renunciation of her love for Newman, on the other hand, seems prototypical in its resemblance to the merely negative self-assertiveness of Alice James, and in the severity of the loss.

A reader familiar with James's central characters will recognize that Newman is permitted an expression of feeling few of the others enjoy, the luxury of losing his temper. Newman's temper comes up as a joke in an early scene with Mrs. Tristram:

> "I don't believe," [Mrs. Tristram] returned, "that you're never angry. A man *ought* to be angry sometimes, and you're neither good enough nor bad enough always to keep your temper."
>
> "I lose it perhaps every five years."
>
> "This time's coming round then," said his hostess. "Before I've known you six months I shall see you in a magnificent rage." (2:44)

The Bellegardes' machinations rouse their daughter Claire from docility to a merely negative assertiveness: the refusal to obey them. And she imagines her departure from their house only in the familiar terms of submissiveness and enforced silence, for she flees to a convent. The Bellegardes do succeed, however, in rousing Newman's fury and he can both recognize that feeling and deliver it from silence.

As he rages over his victimization by the Bellegardes, Newman and his rhetoric are almost swallowed up by melodrama: " 'I want to bring them [the Bellegardes] down—down, down, down! . . . They took me up into a high place and made me stand there for all the world to see me, and then they stole behind me and pushed me into this bottomless pit where I lie howling and gnashing my teeth!' " (2:442). In his fury, he resolves to threaten the Bellegardes with exposure of their crime (Madame de Bellegarde caused the death of her husband when he tried to interfere in Claire's marriage to a rich but depraved nobleman). Although he is ultimately frustrated in his effort to expose the family, Newman experiences his anger intensely and directly enough to put him beyond it and the melodrama of his helpless victimization against which it is directed.

Thus when he goes to view the lifeless exterior of the Carmelite convent in which Claire has immured herself, and expects that the sight will fuel his rage and hatred, he finds instead that "the barren stillness of the place represented somehow his own release from ineffectual desire. It told him the woman within was lost beyond recall. . . . These days and years, on this spot, would always be just so grey and silent. Suddenly from the thought of their seeing him stand there again the charm utterly departed. He would never stand there again; it was a sacrifice as sterile as her own" (2:533). The "charm" of standing literally and figuratively in one place forever has "utterly departed." It is a "sterile sacrifice," neither picturesque, inevitable, nor ennobling. Such willingness altogether to depart from the past is unusual in James's major figures.

While he rests in Notre Dame after viewing the convent, Newman works himself even more fully beyond the rage which would bind him indefinitely to the melodrama in which he has been helpless: "The most unpleasant thing that had ever happened to him had reached its formal conclusion; he had learnt his lesson . . . and could now put away the book.

He leaned his head for a long time on the chair in front of him; when he took it up he felt he was himself again. Somewhere in his soul a tight constriction had loosened. He thought of the Bellegardes; he had almost forgotten them" (2:534). Now his recent experience is "unpleasant," but not teethgnashingly horrible, not the "bottomless pit" into which he had previously felt pushed, emotionally and rhetorically. Newman gains distance on his melodramatic experience by consigning it to fiction—a book that he can now put away— a remoteness reinforced by the fact that Newman is not an avid reader. Throughout the Gothicized portions of the novel, events have been likened to "a page torn out of a romance,"[5] or to "a page torn out of some superannuated unreadable book, with no context in his own experience" (2:478). The effect of these references is to wipe the events from the unliterary Newman's ongoing existence. He returns to his characteristic equanimity: "himself again."

Having fully experienced his anger with the Bellegardes, Newman can be free of them in the most profound sense— free even of the wish to do them harm: "He gave a groan as he remembered what he had meant to do; he was annoyed, yet partly incredulous, at his having meant to do it; the bottom had suddenly fallen out of his revenge. . . . of course he would let the Bellegardes go" (2:534). The untheatrical "of course" which appears before "he would let the Bellegardes go," the charmingly unrighteous "annoyed" response Newman has to his recollected revenge, and the lightly reasoned self-correction, "Such things were really not his game," which follows these in the original edition (*American*, orig. ed., p. 305) provide rhetorical evidence for his escape from melodrama. They also suggest a downright triviality in the revenge, which makes its sacrifice seem all the more satisfying. Because Newman does not lose a valuable realm of experience or an opportunity for growth in what he renounces, his renunciation is less troubling than others in James.[6]

Considering the petty and unsatisfying nature of the revenge he gives up, it is all the more remarkable that Newman is uncertain that he is right to renounce, far less sure than Claire or than Fleda Vetch and Strether are in their decisions to renounce. Newman leaves Notre Dame "not with the elastic step of a man who has won a victory or taken a resolve" (2:534), but like a man whose decision is still subject to change. Newman's imperfectly resolved state emerges most strikingly in the book's last scene as it is described in the original edition. In both editions, Newman cuts his ties to the past and its melodramatizing memories by burning the evidence he has against the Bellegardes, an incriminating letter which constitutes, in effect, a memento of his disastrous love affair. In the original edition, Newman's reconsideration after burning the letter receives the special emphasis accorded a conclusion:

> "It is most provoking," said Mrs. Tristram, "to hear you talk of the 'charge' when the charge is burnt up. Is it quite consumed?" she asked, glancing at the fire.
> Newman assured her that there was nothing left of it.
> "Well then," she said, "I suppose there is no harm in saying that you probably did not make them [the Bellegardes] so very uncomfortable. . . . They believed that, after all, you would never really come to the point. . . . You see they were right."
> Newman instinctively turned to see if the little paper was in fact consumed; but there was nothing left of it.
> (*American*, orig. ed., p. 309)

Newman is permanently temptable, constantly open to a range of impulses and importunities, and still, like Mrs. Tristram, a little furious. That he is emphatically not a man "who ha[d] won a victory or taken a resolve" engages our sympathies for his renunciation all the more. James is laughing: at Newman for his slyly rendered interest in reversing his decision—it shows in the teasingly "little" paper and the forlorn "nothing left of it"; at his own impulses to transform Newman into a noble sacrificial hero; and at our eagerness to have such transformation and such nobility. In neither edition is Newman motivated by Strether's desire to be definitively " 'right' " (22:326).

The largest part of *The American*, title notwithstanding, is devoted to exploring the nineteenth-century female stereotype of victimization and self-sacrifice. Women characters who represent this stereotype are repeatedly the center of James's fiction. In *The American*, as elsewhere, James both represents the stereotype and examines its origins and dynamics as he assesses the costs of the renunciation it produces.

At the death of her corrupt, elderly husband, Claire de Cintré returns home to live with her mother, in whose salon hang "portraits of each of . . . [her] children at the age of ten" (2:181), and who announces to Newman " 'My power . . . is in my children's obedience' " (2:370). James puts forward several possible interpretations of Claire's willingness to submit to her mother's power when Mrs. Tristram informs Newman of the girl's family situation:

> "She suffers from her grim old mother and from the manner in which her elder brother . . . abets and hounds on the Marquise. . . . But I can almost forgive them, because . . . she's simply a saint, and a persecution is all that she needs to bring out what I call her quality."
>
> ". . . But why does she *let* them persecute her? Isn't she, as a married woman, her own mistress?"
>
> "Legally yes, I suppose; but morally no. In France you may never say Nay to your mother, whatever she requires of you. . . . You've simply to obey. The thing has a fine side to it. Madame de Cintré bows her head and folds her wings." (2:109)

Mrs. Tristram, whose excesses of imagination are frequently the butt of the book's satire, wants to romanticize Claire's suffering into nobility, even dove-like saintliness, characteristic ways of construing renunciation in James. She bolsters this interpretation with an ethnic defense based on the absolute authority of the French mother. Newman counteracts this interpretation with a practical, implicitly psychological view which raises questions like: What's wrong with her? Isn't she grown up?

James left the psychological dimension of Claire's relationship with her mother undeveloped in the novel, but later acknowledged its existence and his own inexplicitness about it in an acute bit of self-criticism in the book's preface: "With this lady [Claire], altogether, I recognise, a light plank, too light a plank, is laid for the reader over a dark 'psychological' abyss. The delicate clue to her conduct [renouncing Newman] is never definitively placed in his hand" (*Prefaces*, p. 39). Yet the psychology, which is a planked-over abyss in the preface, is no less real or powerful in the novel for being only semi-visible.

Valentin explains to Newman the roots of his sister's filial submissiveness:

> "After his [Claire's husband's] death his family pounced upon his money, brought a lawsuit against his widow. . . . In the course of the suit some revelations were made as to his private history which my sister found so little to her taste that she . . . washed her hands of all her interests. . . . she . . . at last bought her freedom—obtained my mother's assent to her compromising the suit at the price of a promise. . . . To do anything else whatever, for the next ten years, that might be asked of her—anything, that is, but marry." (2:151–52)

Her strength consists of a resolution not to take—either her husband's money, which would enable her to establish a "house" independent of her family, or a new husband. In exchange for ten years of obedience she receives the "freedom" to refuse: instead of reserving the right to marry whomever she wishes, she reserves the right not to marry if she does not wish to. As in the later decision to reject Newman and enter a convent, her sense of self is defined negatively, through refusals and resistances which appear assertive but actually consolidate her subjugation. Essentially Claire assents to imprisonment in her mother's imagination of her life.

When Claire agrees to her mother's demand that she break her engagement and renounce Newman, he pleads, " 'Complain of her. . . . Tell me all about it . . . and we'll talk it over so satisfactorily that you'll keep your plighted faith' " (2:411). Newman intuits that if Claire could " 'complain' " about her mother, she might be free of her and the composition of life that requires renunciation. But to Newman's demands that she reject her mother's design of her life, Claire responds with stereotypical female passivity: " 'I'm not made for boldness and defiance. . . . I was made to do gladly and gratefully what's expected of me' " (2:416). Not only does she maintain silence and exert no power on behalf of her own imagination of experience, but the very roots of desire for such power have been lost to her. She avoids speaking to her mother about the rumors of family infamy surrounding the death of her father primarily, we infer, because she fears the discovery of something that would make her feel so angry that she would be compelled to reject her mother's control of her life altogether.

After Claire obeys her mother and renounces Newman, she acts against her family's wishes by entering a convent. Her seeming defiance gives the appearance of new instincts for power and independence, but a closer look suggests that she is once again augmenting her identity negatively—through resistance rather than reinvention. The life of a nun duplicates in crucial ways Claire's life at home. It is a second imprisonment in a child's world, in which the choices of the self are once again dependent upon the authority of "Mother Superior." As a nun, the only time Claire can break her silence, in a fitting twist of the plot, is in the regulated anonymity of a wordless chant. When Newman attends a service at the convent in the hope of singling out Claire's voice, he hears the nuns' "impersonal wail" in a passage that throws the windows wide open on the horror of Claire's self-obliteration:

> It began softly, but it presently grew louder, and as it increased it became more of a wail and a dirge. It was the chant of the Carmelite nuns, their only human utterance. . . . It was hideous, it was horrible; as it continued he felt he needed all his self-control. He was growing more agitated, the tears were hot in his eyes. At last . . . the thought came over him that this confused, impersonal wail was all that he or the world she had deserted were ever again to hear [of her]. (2:480–81)

Richard Poirier suggests that James saw Claire de Cintré in the same way that he saw Newman, as one of his "unfixed" or freely expansive characters: "Claire's openness, her capacity for experience, is contrasted explicitly with her mother's stultifying completedness of character."[7] James has Newman pay tribute to Claire's potential for liberating indefiniteness in an adroit description that confirms his distance from the world of the poetic imagination at the same time as it allows him access to its verbal riches: "If it had been his habit to express himself in poetic figures he might have said that in observing her he seemed to see the vague circle sometimes attending the partly-filled disc of the moon" (2:145). Mrs. Tristram explains that in entertaining Newman's proposal of marriage, Claire " 'turned about on a thousand gathered prejudices and traditions as on a pivot and looked where she had never looked till that instant' " (2:179). And yet, the convent's character as a house of constriction and obliteration, evident again when Newman visits the part of the cloister located on the aptly named rue d'Enfer, makes it clear that expectancy and expansiveness are not finally values that Claire embodies.

[Newman] found himself in a part of Paris that he little knew—a region of convents and prisons, of streets bordered by long dead walls and traversed by few frequenters. At the intersection of two of these streets stood the house of the Carmelites—a dull, plain edifice with a blank, high-shouldered defence all round. From without he could see its upper windows, its steep roof and its chimneys. But these things revealed no symptoms of human life; the place looked dumb, deaf, inanimate. The pale, dead, discoloured wall stretched beneath it far down the empty side-street—a vista without a human figure. (2:532)

There are other versions in James of this sinister house with its windows aloft and its "dead . . . wall." One of those already noted is the parentally authorial house of fiction described in the preface to *The Portrait*. Another is the house of the tyrannically parental Osmond which James depicts as having a lethal effect on Isabel in *The Portrait* itself. Still another is Dr. Sloper's house on Washington Square into which Catherine ultimately disappears "for life."

————————WASHINGTON SQUARE————————

Much of the material that appears in *The American* is reworked in *Washington Square* (1880), where Catherine is her father's victim by virtue of being his child. In store for her, he "had usually a little smile, never a very big one. . . . You would have surprised him if you had told him so; but it is a literal fact that he almost never addressed his daughter save in the ironical form" (p. 217). Early in the novel, James comes forward from behind Sloper's debilitating irony, the instrument, in this novel, of parental victimization. "[Catherine] suddenly developed a lively taste for dress: a lively taste is quite the expression to use. . . . Her great indulgence of it was really the desire of a rather inarticulate nature to manifest itself; she sought . . . to make up for her diffidence of speech by a fine frankness of costume" (p. 207). At the heart of the

novel is James's tenderness toward "the desire of a rather inarticulate nature to manifest itself"—toward Catherine's
struggle to locate and deliver into being an independently
imagined self.

James W. Gargano writes that the novella renders the process by which Catherine "acquires selfhood and inner being,"
and shrewdly traces the stages of her growth in her ability to
register anger, however subtly, with Mrs. Penniman and her
father.[8] Gargano's argument is directed at Richard Poirier's
proposition that James identifies for nearly half of the book
with Sloper's ironic treatment of Catherine because he, James,
like her father, finds Catherine vacuous. Poirier, whose analysis of *Washington Square* must be taken into account by anyone
who writes about the book, comments: "To take . . . [Sloper]
throughout simply as a melodramatic figure [that is, a victim-
izer] is to ignore the fact that before the terrible scene on the
Alps, his ironic observation of experience is, with some slight
modification, James's own."[9] Certainly it is true that in passages like the one quoted above, James takes pleasure in his
own verbal irony at Catherine's expense: "a lively taste is quite
the expression to use" about her "fine frankness of costume."
And yet, as Darshan Singh Maini comments, the book is substantially about "the morality of irony."[10]

Millicent Bell suggests that the book's "true subject . . . is
style, in the sense of ways of behavior as well as in the sense
of literary tone."[11] Her observation, like Maini's comment on
irony, points to the work's central dialogue between surface
on the one hand and inwardness or depth on the other. All
of the characters except Catherine are in one way or another
masters of style, of surface display or artful expression, including the rhetorical art of irony. Gargano comments that
Mrs. Penniman's imagination is satirized because it "has no
source in felt experience."[12] That is, it operates entirely at the
surface, as a matter of theatrical performance and posturing,
divorced from the emotion that makes appearances mean-

ingful in more than a decorative sense. Catherine, however, has "a style so mute and motionless as to be almost the surrender of style . . . which derives from an inability to employ any manner dictated by social or literary convention."[13]

Catherine frees James from Sloper's brittle ironies, liberates the work from an excess of surface of the kind that is painfully apparent, for example, in James's own early ironic descriptions of the doctor:

> If he sometimes explained matters more minutely than might seem of use to the patient, he never went so far . . . as to trust to the explanation alone, but always left behind him an inscrutable prescription. There were some doctors that left the prescription without offering any explanation at all; and he did not belong to that class either, which was after all the most vulgar. It will be seen that I am describing a clever man.
>
> (P. 197)

James fussily tacks back and forth here only to produce a pseudocompliment, a labor of wit we feel is disproportionate to the emotional weight of the doctor until he is shown to have an effect on his daughter's emotions. Catherine gives James another place to go, narratively speaking, than mere surface.

> The girl was very happy. She knew not as yet what would come of it; but the present had suddenly grown rich and solemn. . . . Love demands certain things as a right; but Catherine had no sense of her rights; she had only a consciousness of immense and unexpected favours. Her very gratitude for these things had hushed itself; for it seemed to her that there would be something of impudence in making a festival of her secret.
>
> (Pp. 237–38)

Thus James loses interest rather early in identifying with Sloper's cleverness, Catherine's "consciousness" or "inner being" in Gargano's phrase, has grown sufficiently to permit him to play surface against depth.

Though she manages an occasional subterfuge with her father and Aunt Penniman, however, Catherine's essential discomfort with the social arts of speech remains. Not until Maisie Farange and Maggie Verver does James show a character reinventing the meaning of silence by making it an instrument for locating emotion and delivering a self to the world. For Catherine, silence proves severely handicapping to her growth out of Dr. Sloper's house of fiction. Only by articulating her nature, only by forging her felt experience into a social style, could she take supreme imaginative possession of her life.

Bell calls the "rhetoricians" or masters of verbal surface who surround Catherine "melodramatists"; the ironic Sloper is said to use "the weapon of language against the defenseless Catherine."[14] One of the psycho-rhetorical lucidities of *Washington Square* is that it suggests that melodrama, a mode of excess, and irony, a mode of understatement, can be two sides of the same coin. Melodrama is frequently the effect of irony. Insofar as irony is characterized by a sense of superiority and the detached withholding of emotion, exercising the ironic style on a human subject may involve a sense of cruelty and produce a sense of suffering that are melodramatic in their intensity. While it is true that Catherine determines to marry Morris in defiance of her father's wishes, and that she is able to evaluate and finally "place" Mrs. Penniman in the background of her life, she ultimately remains a hostage of the negatively defined melodramatic identity in which her father's brutal ironies have subdued her.

Note the scene in which, years after she has been jilted, Dr. Sloper seeks a promise from his daughter that she will never, even after his death, marry Morris. Considering that it seems clear by now that she intends never to marry Morris, Catherine's response is oddly stubborn: she marshalls all her energy to resist her father, without really confronting him and then setting him aside.

> All her acquired tranquillity and rigidity protested. . . .
> "I can't promise," she simply repeated.
> "You are very obstinate," said the Doctor.
> "I don't think you understand."
> "Please explain, then."
> "I can't explain," said Catherine; "and I can't promise."
>
> (P. 379)

In *The American,* Claire de Cintré makes her mother agree not to force her to marry if she does not wish to, but she fails to secure the agreement in positive forms—that is, permission to marry whomever she chooses. Similarly, although Catherine resists her father's request that she promise not to marry Morris, she does not, to judge by the ending of the novella, secure for herself the sense of freedom to marry anyone else. She is confined by the act of refusal. In Freud's terms, her negation represents "a kind of intellectual acceptance of the repressed [here, perhaps, the desire to make her father superfluous—to her romantic life], while at the same time what is essential to the repression persists."

When James associates Catherine's seemingly mature "tranquillity" with "rigidity," he suggests that her obstinacy before her father derives from some cessation of growth, some hardening in place. He comments wryly, "She knew herself that she was obstinate, and it gave her a certain joy. She was now a middle-aged woman" (p. 379). As her decision to remain in her father's house at the end of the book implies, Catherine would rather stay to resist him than get away from him altogether.

Morris encounters the same obstinately silenced emotion in his last meeting with Catherine. The now aged suitor turns

up again after Sloper's death to urge upon Catherine his proposal of marriage. " 'Ah, you are angry!' cried Morris. . . .
'No, I am not angry [she replied]. Anger does not last that
way for years. But there are other things. Impressions last,
when they have been strong. But I can't talk' " (p. 391). Although her rejection of the requests of both men makes it
appear that she has achieved an identity independent of them,
Catherine's retreat, prefaced with the familiar refrain " 'I can't
talk,' " suggests that there is still some part of her she cannot
quite make contact with and that it therefore is not fully hers.

The two men's encounters with Catherine's resistant silences are but one way in which they are shown, in their relation to her, to be alike. Before Morris jilts her, her feelings
for him and his treatment of her repeat many of the elements
of her father's tyranny. She stands in awe of Morris, "stop-
ping short at a distance that was almost respectful," waiting
"submissively" (p. 305)—her demeanor in most scenes with
her father. And like Dr. Sloper, Morris refuses to take her
seriously, and yet, "Her faith in his sincerity was so complete
that she was incapable of suspecting that he was playing with
her" (p. 313). In the same way, Claire and Newman's romantic
relationship in *The American* duplicates the pattern of authority
and dependence that James has established for Claire's relationship with her family. When Claire sobs, " 'I'm weak—
I'm weak,' " Newman reinforces her submission: " 'All the
more reason why you should give yourself up to me.' " When
he proposes marriage, he offers a singularly constrictive kind
of "safety": " 'With me . . . you'll be as safe—as safe'—and
even in his ardour he hesitated for a comparison—'as safe,'
he said, with a kind of simple solemnity, 'as in your father's
arms' " (2:270). James enjoys his irony here, as do we, as he
seems to sit back waiting to see what comparison will come to
Newman's mind. Safety, of course, is precisely the quality that
Claire seeks in the convent as well, as is apparent when she
tries to redress Newman's horror at her retreat to the Car-

melites with the explanation: " 'You've wrong ideas. It's nothing horrible. It's only peace and safety' " (2:418). And although the Bellegarde residence appalls Newman in part because, significantly, it "answer[s] to . . . [his] conception of a convent" (2:59–60), as a traditional lover, he returns to this image of female dependence when he wonders how Claire can "fail to perceive that his house would have all the security of a convent and none of the dampness" (2:424). That there are no real alternatives for Claire de Cintré and Catherine Sloper to these familial patterns of authority and dependence, not even in romance, confirms that neither of them has departed from the parental house of fiction. James shows their romantic world mirroring the limitations of their psychological development.

Catherine's existence at the end of *Washington Square* essentially conforms to her father and Morris's image of her, an image of devaluation based upon her unsuitability for romance. Maini speaks of "the oedipal sediment of the story": "The soured widower is unconsciously trying to make it impossible for his young daughter to leave that house ever."[15] James reveals that in her later years, Catherine has three opportunities to marry, and that "she averted herself *rigidly*" (emphasis added) from them. In one case, the man "was seriously in love with her" (pp. 374, 375). When Catherine settles for life by herself in Washington Square, James comments with a suggestive use of the architectural metaphor: "Catherine continued to live in her father's house, in spite of its being represented to her that a maiden lady of quiet habits might find a more convenient abode. . . . She liked the earlier structure" (p. 382). She lives a life of recoil, a life necessarily shaped outside of herself by virtue of the pleasure she takes in offering opposition.

Catherine dresses the painful incidents of her life in melodramatic metaphors which, perversely, appear to give her a certain sense of satisfaction:

From her own point of view the great facts of her career were that Morris Townsend had trifled with her affection, and that her father had broken its spring. Nothing could ever alter these facts; they were always there, like her name, her age, her plain face. Nothing could ever undo the wrong or cure the pain that Morris had inflicted on her, and nothing could ever make her feel towards her father as she felt in her younger years. There was something dead in her life. (P. 376)

Catherine's reflections are accurate and moving. But like Fleda Vetch in *The Spoils of Poynton*, she also seems to feel a suspect fondness for her pain, theatrically evoked, presumably "from her own point of view," as "the great facts of her career." This fondness further manifests itself in the alacrity with which the stock melodramatic metaphors of broken springs and living death are represented as coming to Catherine's mind, and the aesthetically pleasing repetitions of syntax by which she is represented as knowing her pain. The parallelism of "Morris Townsend had trifled . . . and . . . her father had broken" is completed by the aesthetically pleasurable series of "nothing could ever" clauses. Her fondness for deprivation is implicit even at the book's beginning when James notes: "Morris Townsend was an object on which . . . [Catherine] found that her imagination could exercise itself indefinitely" (p. 220). The retroactively effective poke at Catherine's imagination for settling on an object as meager as Morris for "indefinite" riches is operative at the end when, for Catherine, "the memory of the most beautiful young man in the world had never faded" (p. 378).

Although she is able to evaluate and reject the reality of Morris, she continues to cherish the memory, and seems to prefer it to any material reality, any other suitor. Despite the affection and sympathy which James expends on her virtually throughout the book, she cannot escape the qualification that James's renouncing characters typically suffer at his hands.

When the portly and balding Morris departs for the last time, "Catherine . . . in the parlour, picking up her morsel of fancy-work, had seated herself with it again—for life as it were" (p. 392). In these words, which govern our final perspective on Catherine, James speaks of feminine surrender to a life of genteel domesticity and fantasy ("fancy" work) in terms of triviality ("morsel") and confinement ("for life"). Refusing participation in her father's savagingly genteel exchanges, she nevertheless concludes with a tableau of gentility. William Veeder writes: "When Catherine at the end assumes the traditional pose of the Heroine-with-her-knitting, we recognize the difference between the conventional significance of this gesture—tranquility, productivity, stability—and her life as it will actually be." The ending consolidates "James' transcendence of the genteel tradition,"[16] not only in its evaluation of the emotional costs of the feminine image prized by the age, but in its evaluation of the dangers of "mere" style: the aestheticizing tendencies that can overtake art, his own included (the phrase "morsel of fancy-work" slightingly refers to such art and also provides an example of it), when it is kept in the drawing room, genteelly apart from felt experience.

THE PORTRAIT OF A LADY

The Portrait of a Lady (1881) presents a heroine with a much richer imagination of what she might have from life than either Claire de Cintré or Catherine Sloper possesses. If we did not find the ending troubling, the book in large measure would have failed in what it was after, a loving exploration of that large, authentically imagined version of experience Emerson called "an original relation to the universe" (*Nature*, p. 7)—a relation that originates with the self. James shows that this American romance of the self is supremely difficult to realize in a social world of other, competing selves. Yet the ending—Isabel's decision to renounce the material of her life to another imagination, her husband's—is made torturously unsettling by James's commitment to the possibilities that have been lost. To accept without ongoing reservation Isabel's decision to return to Osmond is mentally to collapse the spectrum of choices that the book exists to offer to Isabel,[17] and to decline one of the invitations that James's fiction most characteristically extends to its readers, the invitation to restrain easy certainty. Yet granted a dissatisfaction with Isabel's ending, a new tone is needed toward what we might want to call her failure, or her mistake, the things for which Oscar Cargill rightly includes her in "the tradition of the limited heroine."[18] Isabel's case calls for the tenderness reserved for great, if failed, efforts and uncontrollable mistakes.

Like the other works discussed in this study, *The Portrait* demonstrates the justness of undertaking to reclaim James from currently hostile feminist criticism because it strengthens one's impression that James wrote regularly with a profound sensitivity to what it was and very often still is like to be a woman. Isabel Archer is more than incidentally female. The book scrutinizes self-definition or self-origination—what Ralph Touchett calls meeting the requirements of one's (own) imagination—both as an ideal in itself, and as an option for specifically female experience. Nina Baym has noted how few critics, feminist or otherwise, have focused on the woman's theme in *The Portrait*, or discussed "the relation of Isabel's story to the woman's movement," which preoccupied the social conscience and the literature of the period in which the novel first appeared. Focusing in illuminating detail on changes that James made in the original 1881 edition for the New York edition in 1908, Baym concludes that James swerved from his initial intention of showing Isabel's failed attempt to be the "new woman."[19] Yet, as much as the first text, the later *Portrait* mourns the melodramatic imbalance of power in human relationships with which feminist thinking most concerns itself and the difficulty posed from within, by a woman's relationship with herself. Thus James wrote that the "deep difficulty braved" was not only concentrating on the heroine, rather than on the "heroine's satellites, especially the male," but making the center of the novel the story of Isabel's "relation to herself" (*Prefaces*, pp. 50, 51). Such independence to which Isabel at first aspires is unattainable not only because of the existence of others, who constitute society and exert pressure on her, but because of conditions within Isabel herself. The feminist emphasis of the book, then, arises most powerfully out of Isabel's conflicting attitudes toward power: her desire for self-origination on the one hand and, on the other, her attraction to dependency. This vacillation makes her vulnerable to Osmond's tyranny, as it makes *The Portrait* an uncannily perceptive study of female consciousness. The point is less that Isabel is deficient than that, given the powerlessness women frequently feel, the challenge of self-origination could not easily be met by any woman, even one as generously conceived as Isabel is by James.

Most critics writing on Isabel's return to Osmond believe that Isabel ultimately triumphs, that she takes authorial charge of her life. Poirier credits Isabel with the status of an inverted Emersonian self-creator: "In effect she tells the reader, to borrow from 'The Transcendentalist,' that 'you think me the child of my circumstances: I make my circumstance,'—including, one might add, 'my own misery.' "[20] Laurence Holland argues that Isabel is the principal authorial figure in *The Portrait* because she performs certain authorial offices "which are shared by a number of characters in the novel but which are realized chiefly in . . . [her] destiny." One of the offices Holland singles out as crucial for establishing the identity of the principal figure of imagination is the assumption of responsibility for "arrangements of matters [pertaining to plot, character, structure, and the like] which he [or she] did not initially control or possess."[21] Yet to argue that Isabel's decision to return to Osmond's mansion represents an assumption of responsibility for "arrangements . . . which . . . [she] did not initially control or possess" is to disregard the claustrophobic and elegiac tone of the last part of the book, the implications of the book's title, and the logical extensions of the similarities between James and Osmond about which Holland himself talks at some length.[22]

Foremost among the competing authorial acts and authorial visions which constitute the plot of *The Portrait* are those of Ralph Touchett and Gilbert Osmond.[23] The two conceive of authorship in very different ways, and the differences substantiate James's conflicts about what it means to be authorial. Ralph's idea is to launch Isabel, whom he regards essentially as his material: " 'I should like to put a little wind in her sails,' " to set her afloat on her own, he explains to his dying father to persuade him to endow Isabel with half his fortune. " 'She's entirely independent of me. . . . But I should like to do something for her. . . . I should like to make her rich. . . . I call people rich when they're able to meet the requirements of their imagination. . . . If she has an easy income she'll never have to marry for a support. . . . She wishes to be free, and your bequest will make her free' " (3:260–61). The freedom Ralph wants to give to Isabel is the power to be the supreme imaginer of her experience. To his father's inquiry about what " 'good' " he will get for himself from his arrangement, Ralph replies, " 'I shall get just the good . . . I wished to put into Isabel's reach—that of having met the requirements of my imagination' " (3:265). Ralph's fulfillment depends upon Isabel's vitality as a "germ"—her possession of what James called "the germinal property and authority" (*Prefaces*, p. 44) of an author's character. The young Touchett wants to watch Isabel take off on her own, in the self-creating manner James repeatedly admired in his subjects in the prefaces, although the kind of authorship represented by Ralph will later suffer qualification because his absence from the design he promotes makes it liable to unravel.

Osmond represents the other psychology of fiction outlined by James in the prefaces. He corresponds to the part of James that wants, tyrannically, to discipline the subject in the house of fiction or to possess it from a window of the house. Osmond's mansion, to which Isabel returns at the end of the novel, is also James's house of fiction in the novel's preface. The similarities have been noted before. "The house of fiction has . . . windows . . . mere holes in a dead wall. . . . at each of them stands a figure with a pair of eyes, or at least with a field-glass . . . the posted presence of the watcher . . . the consciousness of the artist" (*Prefaces*, p. 46). During her fireside vigil, Isabel meditates on her marriages: "She had taken all the first steps in the purest confidence, and then she had suddenly found the infinite vista of a multiplied life to be a dark, narrow alley with a dead wall at the end" (4:189). And later, "Osmond's beautiful mind . . . seemed to peep down from a small high window and mock at her" (4:196). Ultimately, it is Osmond's imagination, not Ralph or Isabel's own, which takes command of the novel and of Isabel herself.

When Lydia Touchett telegraphs Gardencourt with the news of Isabel's imminent arrival, she limits her description of the girl to " 'quite independent,' " although the party at Gardencourt is unsure whether this is meant " 'in a moral or in a financial sense' " (3:13–14). Before acquiring the elder Touchett's legacy, Isabel appears to be the source of her own quite spirited independence. She rejects Lord Warburton's proposal of marriage, for instance, on the strength of her own resources, both moral and financial. Ralph mulls over Isabel's apparent autonomy and the more dependent circumstances of most women:

It was a fine free nature; but what was she going to do with herself? This question was irregular, for with most women one had no occasion to ask it. Most women did with themselves nothing at all; they waited, in attitudes more or less gracefully passive, for a man to come that way and furnish them with a destiny. Isabel's originality was that she gave one an impression of having intentions of her own. (3:87)

Isabel cares about her capacity as a woman to invent and give shape to her own life: "Henrietta, for Isabel, was chiefly a proof that a woman might suffice to herself and be happy. . . . [Isabel] held that a woman ought to be able to live to herself, in the absence of exceptional flimsiness" (3:71). And when Caspar Goodwood accuses her of refusing to marry him because she is planning to marry someone else, she flashes back " 'I don't need the aid of a clever man to teach me how to live. I can find it out for myself' " (3:223).

Ralph nonetheless fears that at some point, Isabel may " 'have to marry for a support,' " and he assumes, fatally, that it is possible to give independence as a gift. In fact, it is just when Isabel comes into the inheritance, and is therefore most capable of independence and freedom, that her allegiance to them falters. She sees her money specifically in terms of power, but she regards that power ambivalently: "The girl presently made up her mind that to be rich was a virtue because it was to be able to *do*, and that to do could only be sweet. It was the graceful contrary of the stupid side of weakness— especially the feminine variety. . . . The acquisition of power made her serious; she scrutinized her power with a kind of tender ferocity, but she was not eager to exercise it" (3:301). While the unaccustomed opportunity "to *do*" and to be strong appeals to Isabel—not long after inheriting the money she makes use of it to travel—her hesitation to "exercise" her power reflects a predisposition toward powerlessness which the wealth actually stimulates. She tells Ralph, " 'A large fortune means freedom, and I'm afraid of that. . . . one must keep thinking; it's a constant effort. I'm not sure it's not a greater happiness to be powerless' " (3:320). She finds not doing restful, a treacherous relief from the " 'constant effort' " of thinking how to make her own life. Isabel's anxiety about having power causes her to make a marriage in which she has none.

Isabel's response to Osmond's declaration of love confirms her fear of power, and anticipates the powerless reality of her marriage:

> The tears came into her eyes: this time they obeyed the sharpness of the pang that suggested to her somehow the slipping of a fine bolt—backward, forward, she couldn't have said which. . . . What made her dread great was precisely the force which, as it would seem, ought to have banished all dread— the sense of something within herself, deep down, that she supposed to be inspired and trustful passion. It was there like a large sum stored in a bank—which there was a terror in having to begin to spend. If she touched it, it would all come out.
>
> (4:18)

Isabel feels confused about whether marriage and "passion" correspond to a bolt slipping backward or forward—and she seems to fear getting free as much as she does being locked up. The idea of imprisonment has an appeal for her; it saves her from the "terror" of "spend[ing]." An old and tired figure for orgasm, the financial metaphor is revitalized by being made to echo the overall concerns of the book: Isabel does inherit a "large sum" to store up and to spend. As Isabel fantasizes it, spending may lead to bankruptcy if, once she touches it, she lets it "all come out." The terms of the sexual and financial metaphor, carried by her fearful imagination to their extreme—spending "all"—represent a fantasy of powerless destruction. Amidst the confusions expressed in the passage, Isabel cannot tell whether marrying Osmond will protect her from poverty or precipitate it, whether sexual "spending" is a sign of "trustful passion" or a prelude to total loss. Like Alice James, Isabel is trapped in her melodramatic metaphors of immobilized confinement on the one hand and total loss of control on the other, helpless at either devastating extreme.

Eventually Isabel realizes that she chose to bankrupt herself, without even enjoying the power and gain that ordinarily accompany spending, by making a marriage in which she gave the money and power all away. In the famous vigil during which the torments and pressures of this marriage force a clearing in her consciousness and the narrative, Isabel is able to recognize that she felt ill at ease with the power conferred by the money: "As she looked back at the passion of those full weeks [when Osmond courted her] she perceived in it a kind of maternal strain—the happiness of a woman who felt that she was a contributor, that she came with charged hands. . . . At bottom her money had been a burden, had been on her mind, which was filled with the desire to transfer the weight of it" (4:192–93).

In her fear of her own power Isabel makes a marriage that is metaphorically a dungeon: "Those four walls . . . were to surround her for the rest of her life," a dark, claustral dwelling in which she is spied upon from above by a jailor—"Osmond's beautiful mind gave it neither light nor air; Osmond's beautiful mind indeed seemed to peep down from a small high window" (4:196). She sees her husband as a kind of Gothic villain, leading her life "downward and earthward, into realms of restriction and depression where the sound of other lives, easier and freer, was heard as from above. . . . it was as if Osmond deliberately, almost malignantly, had put the lights out one by one" (4:189–90). Isabel does not perceive that while she may have come to the marriage as a mother, she lives in it, having given away her power, very like a daughter, very much, in fact, like Osmond's little girl Pansy. At one point, she even realizes that "the sight of her interest in her cousin [Ralph] stirred her husband's rage as if Osmond had locked her into her room—which she was sure was what he wanted to do" (4:202).

Several critics have done important work on melodrama in James,[24] among which Poirier's position is representative:

melodrama results when characters confront "the reality of mystery and evil," "forces over which they have no control."[25] In the terms of my discussion, the loss of control occurs when characters become helplessly caught in the fictions of others. Manfred Mackenzie, writing on melodrama in *The Portrait*, denies that "Osmond [is] the monster that . . . [chapter 42, Isabel's vigil] or any summary of the plot might suggest," and he notes that other characters in the book see Osmond as limited, but distinctly human, not infernal. Mackenzie asks: "Why does Chapter XLII [from which the quotes above are taken] look like melodrama? Why does Isabel seem to experience the same terror of Osmond as Pansy when, unlike Pansy, she is hardly an *'ingenue* in a French play'?" (3:401). He later notes "a very close identification of Isabel with Pansy—long prepared for, it is one of the novel's most brilliant developments."[26] These observations, suggestive in ways I don't think Mackenzie intended, imply a connection between melodrama and childhood feelings of helplessness. Rather than a reflection of a morally absolute drama of good and evil located outside of the self, melodrama may be regarded as the product of a state of mind, a response to a sense of entrapment and helplessness that resembles the response of a child: overwhelmed terror. In such circumstances, the powerful figures that preside over the imagination might naturally loom as threatening as monsters, as they do in a child's imagination, and as Osmond does in Pansy and Isabel's.

Pansy represents a model of female submissiveness and victimization familiar from *The American* and *Washington Square*, but one which is painfully exaggerated here: "She was evidently impregnated with the idea of submission, which was due to any one who took the tone of authority; and she was a passive spectator of the operation of her fate" (3:337–38); "She would easily be mystified, easily crushed: her force would be all in knowing when and where to cling" (4:27). Even when Osmond requires her to give up the suitor she loves, her training in obedience has been so thorough that renunciation is not only a last resort, but a satisfaction. "She was prepared to give up her lover. This might seem an important step toward taking another, but for Pansy, evidently, it failed to lead in that direction. She felt no bitterness toward her father; . . . there was only the sweetness of fidelity to Edward Rosier, and a strange, exquisite intimation that she could prove it better by remaining single than even by marrying him" (4:257). Like Catherine Sloper and Fleda Vetch, she relishes loss and finds pleasure—"a strange, exquisite intimation"—in renunciation. Osmond continues to suggest suitors, and Pansy refuses to accept any of them, a form of merely negative self-assertion that will hold her in her father's fiction indefinitely. In banishing Pansy, for her resistance, to semiimprisonment in the convent where she was boarded and educated as a child, Osmond thinks of himself as putting the "finishing touches" on "a precious work of art" (4:349). Isabel, too, is ultimately reduced to the status of a work of art by another artist.

Isabel's attachment to her stepdaughter is complex. When Pansy refuses to accompany Isabel out of the convent to a freedom that has not been authorized by her father, Isabel promises to return for her, though she is on her way to Gardencourt and a life potentially free of Osmond's control. Her desire "to be more for the child than the child was able to be for herself" (4:161), to help her hold out against Osmond's tyranny better than she could alone, seems generous. But if the wish to help Pansy in this way sets her kind of mothering admirably apart from Madame Merle's, it is also compromisingly substitutive. That is, Isabel's return to Osmond to protect Pansy functions as a substitute for protecting herself by staying away. Her fondness for the child indirectly expresses an attachment to the most dependent parts of herself, and becomes a way of shielding and cherishing her own powerlessness, rather than overcoming it. Her interest in Pansy's marriage, her concern that Pansy make an unmanipulated and satisfying choice, can also be seen as an effort to remake the conditions of her own marriage. Isabel's relationship to Pansy ultimately calls forth a profoundly debilitating expenditure of energy. It allows her to go through the motions of protecting herself from Osmond on a symbolic level, with the result that she does not protect herself from him well enough to escape.

James alludes to this problematic dimension of Isabel's affection for Pansy when he implies that Isabel can find no other compelling reasons to return to Osmond.

> "I don't see why you promised little Miss Osmond to go back" [Henrietta, often the voice of the reader's skepticism, queries].
> "I'm not sure I myself see now," Isabel replied, "But I did then."
> "If you've forgotten your reason perhaps you won't return." . . .
> "In default of a better [reason] my having promised will do," Isabel suggested. (4:397–98)

Even before she makes the promise to Pansy the ostensible justification for her return to Osmond, Isabel thinks of the girl as her principal reason for preserving the marriage when James suggests there may not be any: "Her sense of the girl's dependence [on her] was more than a pleasure; it operated as a definite reason when motives threatened to fail her" (4:161).

Isabel's difficulty in producing reasons and motives for her desire to preserve her marriage is reminiscent of Catherine's inability to explain her feelings to her father and Morris. It is a kind of silence, which suggests that Isabel cannot definitively leave Osmond because she cannot articulate, or recognize, all that she feels about him. When, for example, Isabel communes with herself about her marriage in chapter 42, the note of outrage or even of indignation is hardly present. She only neutrally observes that her husband had "said to her one day that she had too many ideas and that she must get rid of them. . . . What he had meant had been the whole thing—

her character, the way she felt, the way she judged" (4:194–95). Although, as far as Isabel knows at this point, she has chosen Osmond freely, and although she feels that she may even have deceived him when he was courting her by not revealing her character fully, it nevertheless seems strange that she does not dispute his right to efface her. Her most heated thought is "He took himself so seriously; it was something appalling" (4:196). This is not the same thing as Isabel thinking that it appalls *her*. Her feelings about the marriage are registered in aesthetically pleasurable repetitions whose salient feature is their unruffled emotional control: "She could live it over again, the incredulous terror with which she had taken the measure of her dwelling. . . . It was the house of darkness, the house of dumbness, the house of suffocation" (4:196).

Our horror here derives not least from the perfect parallelism James has Isabel—like Catherine Sloper before her—display at such a moment. Isabel's inner voice, like Alice James's journal voice, seems unable to register many of the emotions that someone in her place could reasonably be presumed to feel. Her inability to "take it personally" protects her from becoming angry with Osmond in the same way that Claire de Cintré's failure to react to the rumors surrounding her father's death protects her from becoming angry with her mother.

Another striking instance of Isabel's inability to feel emotion, which the context would seem to dictate, occurs when the Countess Gemini, Osmond's sister, informs her that Osmond and Madame Merle were once lovers and have now betrayed her. Isabel feels scarcely any emotion on her own account: " 'It seems very wonderful,' she murmured; and in this bewildering impression she had almost lost her sense of being personally touched by the story" (4:370). As the Countess recounts Osmond's affair with Madame Merle, Isabel feels emotions almost exclusively on behalf of Madame Merle and Osmond's long-dead first wife:

> "My poor sister-in-law, in her grave, couldn't help herself, and the real mother [of Pansy—Madame Merle], to save *her* skin, renounced all visible property in the child."
>
> "Ah, poor, poor, woman!" cried Isabel, who herewith burst into tears. It was a long time since she had shed any; she had suffered a high reaction from weeping. But now they flowed with an abundance. . . .
>
> "It's very kind of you to pity her!" . . . [the Countess] discordantly laughed. "Yes indeed, you have a way of your own—!"
>
> "He must have been false to his wife—and so very soon!" said Isabel with a sudden check.
>
> "That's all that's wanting—that you should take up *her* cause!" the Countess went on. (4:366–67)

When Isabel subsequently encounters Madame Merle at Pansy's convent, she allows herself a moment of personal reaction, but refuses to put it into words: "There was a moment during which, if she had turned and spoken [to Madame Merle], she would have said something that would hiss like a lash. But she closed her eyes, and then the hideous vision dropped" (4:379). We witness the familiar Jamesian spectacle of emotion transformed into silence, a silence which in this novel results in a loss of self. Between Isabel's own exploitation and her "lash[ing]" of Madame Merle, James prefers the former, the less sinister on Isabel's part: suffering is always the easier of the two faces of melodrama for him to accept. It is to Isabel's credit that she refuses to make her "hideous vision" a reality. And James does grant a vengeful aspect to her silence: "Isabel's only revenge was to be silent still—to leave Madame Merle in this unprecedented situation. . . . Isabel would never accuse her, never reproach her; perhaps because she never would give her the opportunity to defend herself" (4:379–80). Nevertheless, Isabel's substantial repudiation of personal emotion is made suspicious by the language of blindness: "She closed her eyes, and then the hideous vision dropped."

One of the signal ways in which James exhibited his protagonists as special was by showing that they were capable of empathically imagining themselves in the place of other characters. Unlike their fellow actors, who are fixed within the confines of their own sensibilities, these characters can get outside of themselves. Yet Isabel's exercise of empathy with Madame Merle and Osmond's first wife results in an absence from herself that seems as evasive as it does admirable. It is this inability to ground her responses and her empathy in a personal self that causes her imprisonment in Osmond's oedipal fiction of marriage.

Isabel's return to Rome is precipitated by the reappearance of her American suitor Caspar Goodwood.

> "Do you know where you're drifting?" Henrietta pursued.
> . . .
> "No, I haven't the least idea, and I find it very pleasant not to know. A swift carriage, of a dark night, rattling with four horses over roads that one can't see—that's my idea of happiness."
> Mr. Goodwood certainly didn't teach you to say such things as that—like the heroine of an immoral novel," said Miss Stackpole. "You're drifting to some great mistake." (3:235)

It is tempting to view Isabel's fantasy as emblematic of her desire for an open, unplanned, improvisable future. But her insistence in the passage on not seeing, her determination to be blind and, like Pansy, agentless in the operation of her fate, implies an ideal of helplessness. Henrietta correctly suspects Isabel's titillated passivity in this abduction fantasy of a woman mysteriously carried along through the darkness on unseen and unknown roads, and liking it. The fantasy has a Gothic resonance. In the Gothic mode, the combination of terror with eroticism in the persecution of innocent females relieved the women of responsibility for their sexual impulses. Thus Isabel can enjoy fantasizing about her life as an abduction, but when Caspar materializes, ready to enable her to turn the fantasy into a chosen sexual reality, it would seem that she is terrified of assenting and of thereby taking responsibility—no longer agentless—for the attraction he exerts over her even when she finds him boring and oppressive.

Many critics accept Caspar as the embodiment of virility, and view Isabel's rejection of him, especially in the garden scene at the end of the novel, as proof of her sexual unresponsiveness.[27] While the novel certainly provides grounds for believing that Isabel is afraid of sexuality, James presents Caspar as the last man who could alter that fear. His symbolic hardness and stiffness of carriage, to which James calls frequent attention, convey unnaturalness and hostility as much as sexual presence. His appearance is associated with images of armor and concussion:

> His jaw was too square and set and his figure too straight and stiff: these things suggested a want of easy consonance with the deeper rhythms of life. . . . she saw the different fitted parts of him as she had seen, in museums and portraits, the different fitted parts of armoured warriors. (3:165)

> She came back . . . to her old sense that he was naturally plated and steeled, armed essentially for aggression.
> (3:219–20)

> His figure [had] a kind of bareness and bleakness which

made the accident of meeting it in memory or in apprehension
a peculiar concussion.   (4:280)

In creating the sinuous figure of Prince Amerigo in *The Golden
Bowl*, James demonstrated that he did not believe that male
sexuality was by definition rigid and concussive; it could have
its own kind of suppleness.

In the imagery that he reserves for Caspar, James reveals
a sensitivity to the characteristic sexual scenarios to which
women's feelings of powerlessness frequently reduce them,
plots that are impoverished even when they appear to be romantic. Caspar's sexuality, stereotypically romantic, actually
qualifies him as a kind of rapist lover: he inspires in Isabel
sexual fantasies of powerlessness and forced penetration. His
passion "lifted her off her feet, while the very taste of it, as
of something potent, acrid and strange, forced open her set
teeth" (4:434). A fantasy of drowning takes shape when Caspar presses upon her "his kiss . . . like white lightning": "While
she took it, she felt each thing in his hard manhood that had
least pleased her, each aggressive fact of his face, his figure,
his presence, justified of its intense identity and made one
with this act of possession. So had she heard of those wrecked
and under water following a train of images before they sink"
(4:436). The notable point about these images is not that
drowning and dying are traditional metaphors for sexual
passion, nor that Isabel is sexually fearful. The point is that
Isabel has every reason to fear an instance of sexuality—
whether it is spending with Osmond, or drowning and dying
with Caspar—which demands to be seen as a form of self-
enfeeblement or self-extinction. The assumption has been that
such fantasies would be appropriate and unthreatening if Isabel was not "frigid" to begin with. But James has given Caspar
a sexual identity which justifies Isabel's fearful associations of
eroticism with violence.

Through the imagery of spending and drowning, I believe
James was attempting to evoke the fantasies of powerlessness
and damage which often dominate female sexuality, and, by

evoking them, to question their appropriateness. In questioning the metaphors, James was also questioning that vision of human relations, especially sexual relations, based on domination and passivity. What was necessary above all to keep sexual possession from becoming an extinction of self for the woman was a sense of self-possession which would ultimately make the very metaphor of possession obsolete. The implicit discomfort with such inherited metaphors for sexuality, which seems operative also in the box imagery of *In the Cage*, suggests a sensibility inclined toward conceiving new, collaborative possibilities for human relations.

When he reappears after Ralph's death, Caspar first appeals to Isabel by offering her an existence absolutely without restraint or responsibility to others, the Emersonian freedom of a self-designed life. In the early parts of the book, this ideal attracts Isabel. She contemplates her character in terms that convey typically Romantic attitudes of self-regard, and compares herself to a garden in a potentially Romantic metaphor of organic growth:

> It often seemed to her that she thought too much about herself.
> . . . She was always planning out her development, desiring her perfection, observing her progress. Her nature had, in her conceit, a certain garden-like quality, a suggestion of perfume and murmuring boughs, of shady bowers and lengthening vistas, which made her feel that introspection was, after all, an exercise in the open air, and that a visit to the recesses of one's spirit was harmless when one returned from it with a lapful of roses. (3:72)

Yet Isabel's confidence in her "germinal property" is conveyed through the image of a European garden, carefully tended and tamed, full of such flowers as roses and, perhaps, a Pansy or two (Pansy's name is I think one of the book's crueler ironies), which suggest not so much independent Romantic growth as a high degree of cultivation. James thus makes Isabel use an image by means of which she undercuts her ideal. It is part of the novel's critique of the ideas about the self represented by American Romanticism that Isabel thereafter comes in a conscious way to a more balanced and largely considered point of view toward the possibilities of unlimited growth and individual power. "The desire for unlimited expansion had been succeeded in her soul by the sense that life was vacant without some private duty that might gather one's energies to a point" (4:82). By the time Caspar makes his last appearance, to press Isabel to choose a life designed only by the personal self, she has accepted the principle of the "magnificent form" (4:356) behind the individual choice of marriage.

Sublimely unaware of the impossibility of giving freedom by fiat (as Ralph's gift has shown), and of the change in perspective through which the ideas of freedom and commitment have passed in the book during his absence, Caspar offers Isabel a means of escape from Osmond. Caspar has been encouraged to take care of Isabel by Ralph, when Ralph knows he is about to die, and some of the qualities of Ralph's early bequest of freedom to Isabel necessarily undergo retroactive qualification in the ultimate development James gives Caspar's character. " 'Why shouldn't we be happy—when it's here before us, when it's so easy? . . . We can do absolutely as we please; to whom under the sun do we owe anything? . . . The world's all before us—and the world's very big. I know something about that' " (4:434–35). With an appreciative grasp of American cultural connections, James makes the commercial Goodwood the ultimate spokesman for the radically individualistic vein in American Romanticism in a passage that grafts Emerson onto Milton. Although for Caspar the world before them is Eden itself, or that version of paradise that Emerson thought could be achieved by every man through an "original relation" to experience in which the self discovered its potential infinitude, the echoes of *Paradise Lost* identify Caspar and Isabel with our sinning Biblical and literary ancestors, placing them in a fallen world in which inherited nature takes precedence over originality. The self is small, not limitless, hemmed in by and indebted to others, not independent. This is true not least of all for Caspar, upon whom James plays the trick of making him owe his language to Milton.

Yet while Caspar's language seems naively unconscious of itself, and the claims to freedom voiced in that language seem irresponsible, Isabel's retreat from his offer, as James describes it, is equally troubling. Isabel, perhaps justifiably, fears Caspar's "white lightning" kiss:

> When darkness returned she was free. She never looked about her; she only darted from the spot. There were lights in the windows of the house; they shone far across the lawn. In an extraordinarily short time—for the distance was considerable—she had moved through the darkness (for she saw nothing) and reached the door. Here only she paused. She looked all about her; she listened a little; then she put her hand on the latch. She had not known where to turn; but she knew now. There was a very straight path. (4:436)

"When darkness returned she was free": to Isabel's perplexed vision, darkness is freedom. Twice James associates her flight with willed blindness: "She never looked about her," and "she saw nothing." When Osmond proposed, Isabel did not know whether to associate passion with a bolt slipping forward or backward, and was not sure which she preferred. When she flees Caspar, she chooses to latch herself in, and almost immediately returns to Rome and confinement in Osmond's house of darkness.

Newman, and James himself, charm us by eschewing moral certitude. The reassuring moral certainty implied by "straight path," with its automatically sanctifying echo of scripture, makes it seem that Isabel rejects Caspar because he confuses her. Her preoccupation with choosing what is right diminishes her insofar as it simplifies her response to what is. In offering to take her away, Caspar has supposed that Isabel cares little " 'for the look of the thing, for what people will say' " (4:434). But Henrietta intuits that Osmond's hold over Isabel is that " 'You won't confess that you've made a mistake.' " Isabel's response is admirable—" 'One must accept one's deeds!' "— yet her accompanying statements sound like nothing more weighty than face-saving: " 'I can't publish my mistake. . . . I married him before all the world' " (4:284). Ralph too, on his deathbed, concludes that Isabel is overly concerned both with being right and appearing to be right. "He murmured simply. 'You must stay here.' 'I should like to stay—as long as seems right,' [she replied]. 'As seems right—as seems right?' He repeated her words. 'Yes, you think a great deal about that.' 'Of course one must,' she said" (4:416). Isabel's willingness to renounce the claims of the personal self in order to be right at any cost anticipates Strether's resolve at the end of *The Ambassadors* " 'not, out of the whole affair, to have got anything for myself' " in order " 'to be right.' "

The Portrait represents a major leap forward from *The American* and *Washington Square* in James's ability to manage the dialectic between surface and depth, between social forms and expectations, on the one hand, and inner desires on the other, between an externally formulated style and a naked Emersonian originality. Though surfaces and forms, as in the earlier books, are associated with deceitful characters, they are no longer viewed as necessarily inauthentic. When read properly, surfaces tell the truth. It is in this light that James's reputation as a founder of realism can be understood, even though so much of his work seems to draw upon allegorical, psychological, and metaphysical resources. If adherents of realism believed that life's reality resided in its surfaces, James qualifies as a realist because of his ability to show what consciousness makes of surface details—things seen, heard, touched. In speaking of James as a psychological realist, it may even be appropriate to refer to the "date of conscious-ness."

As Madame Merle puts it in her celebrated exchange with Isabel on how best to express the self in society, whether by going naked or by wearing clothes, " 'I've a great respect for *things*! One's self—for other people—is one's expression of one's self; and one's house, one's furniture, one's garments, the books one reads, the company one keeps—these things are all expressive' " (3:287–88). The great so-called recognition scenes in *The Portrait* and *The Ambassadors*, though we might ultimately want to call them social epiphanies, are triumphs in the realistic mode, triumphs for the world of things. Only through the world of things can Isabel have her epiphany, the "sudden flicker of light," (4:165) that signals a moment of revelation or insight. Thus Isabel's recognition that Os-mond and Madame Merle are closer friends than she knew grows out of the realistic handling of their mere physical placement: Madame Merle standing, Osmond sitting in her presence, a breach of decorum unless the couple is intimate. Similarly, Strether's recognition that Chad and Madame de Vionnet are lovers depends upon his ability to read surfaces, here, realistic details of clothing—the French woman's lack of a shawl or other nighttime apparel, and her possession of a vacationer's pink parasol—from which he deduces the ex-istence of "a quiet retreat . . . at which they had been spending the twenty-four hours" (22:265). Maggie's recognition too is associated with a simple change in physical positioning—she waits for her husband's return from Matcham at their house, rather than at her father's.

Although Madame Merle qualifies her assertion of the im-portance of social surfaces and forms by saying " 'One's self—*for other people*—is one's expression of one's self' " (emphasis added), the book implies that the forms one selects to express oneself may also make one's identity *for oneself*. John Carlos Rowe acutely points out that James's brilliance as a critic of the Romantic ideal of transcendence was his belief that depth could and must be wed to surface, that the self could learn to speak in society. The question is whether Isabel achieves this fluency. Rowe notes that, initially, "Isabel has been caught in the fiction of a self complete in its own right, remote from the destructive elements of time, change, and social relation," but he argues that "the new Isabel, who emerges from the fireside contemplation in Chapter 42, recognizes that social responsibility, unlike blind duty or romantic escapism, is the expression of one's self in relation to others."[28] Consider, however, the way in which the dialectic between social forms and personal authenticity is resolved in *The Golden Bowl*. Though Maggie, like Isabel, maintains the form of marriage, Maggie ends up with something more than mere form, while the conclusion of *The Portrait*, with its air of elegiac closure and blind choice, suggests that Isabel does not. Infusing a luxuriant Emersonianism with great formal grace, Maggie makes social responsibility coexist with originality or personal design. The forms are a kind of clothing by means of which her personal self can express and achieve its desires, not a cross on which these are crucified.

Osmond desires "the observance of . . . [the] magnificent form" (4:356) of marriage, regardless, apparently, of its substance. Although it is tempting to think that, in returning to Osmond, Isabel will be able to have an original relation to the form of marriage, all efforts at independence are doomed in Osmond's presence. What expression of self is possible with someone for whom "The real offence, as she ultimately perceived, was her having a mind of her own at all. Her mind was to be his—attached to his own like a small garden-plot to a deer-park" (4:200). What remains for Isabel is the prospect of showing Osmond that she can go on by resisting him even as she lives with him. Linda Ray Pratt argues that James rejected the myth of Adamic innocence, and that as a result his female characters profited from occupying a material world of change and social relations. She sees Isabel's return to Osmond in positive terms, as neither a renunciation nor a retreat, and concludes that Isabel's "understanding of Osmond's nature and of her own egotistical deception frees her from Osmond's moral and spiritual influence." Yet how free is Isabel of Osmond's influence if her freedom consists of "her unwillingness to continue as an obedient agent for Osmond . . . [as] illustrated in her refusal to further promote the Warburton-Pansy affair, and by her defiant trip to England"?[29] The identity she constitutes in this way is a negative of Osmond's identity, rather than her own independent self. She lives in neither the world of personal agency nor the world of social relations.

Portrait of a Lady was, and still is, a common title in the tradition of portraiture, and Osmond is a collector.[30] In the following much-noted passage, Isabel is that typed and anonymous figure of the book's title, a lady—both a woman enclosed by forms and a formally posed subject of traditional painting: "Now, at all events, framed in the gilded doorway, she struck our young man [Ned Rosier] as the picture of a gracious lady" (4:105).[31] Ralph, on a later visit, notes that "There was something fixed and mechanical in the serenity painted on . . . [Isabel's face]; this was not an expression, Ralph said—it was a representation" (4:142). Isabel is never called a lady by James in the preface. The word is Osmond's way of imagining her: "His egotism had never taken the crude form of desiring a dull wife; this lady's intelligence was to be a silver plate" (4:79). By showing Isabel as the figure in the book's title, both portrait and lady, in relation to Osmond, James suggests that Osmond has become the chief imaginer of her life, she his work of art.

Ultimately, Isabel is in danger of being appropriated by Osmond's mind, and becoming merely a figment of a man's imagination: "She had not been mistaken about the beauty of . . . [Osmond's] mind. . . . She had lived with it, she had

lived *in* it almost—it appeared to have become her habitation."
(4:194). Absorbed back into Osmond's imagination, she will
have been simply evaporated, the ultimate blow to her effort
to constitute her own identity as a token for a human being,
a woman, and a literary character.

Ralph's death suggests that the conception of authorship
which he embodied has given way to the opposing conception
of authorship embodied by Osmond. James regards it as a
necessary though regrettable demise. James applauds Ralph
for promoting and then releasing Isabel, but he distrusts
Ralph's failure to be accountable for what happens to her and
the plot—his failure to make his imagination predominate.
The garden author abdicates too much responsibility. Osmond's virtue in this respect, as it is also the source of his
tyranny, is his willingness to bring back for discipline the
"house-dog of a temper above confinement," as James insists
it must be returned. Osmond accepts ultimate accountability
for both Isabel's life and the plot. Yet James's own act of
imagination escapes this degree of tyranny and allows the fiction a release from such melodrama precisely by fostering the
ambiguities that call into question the purity of the renunciations. In these ambiguities there is also an invitation to
James's central characters to imagine themselves out of melodrama.

—3—
Ambassadorial Consciousness

A LTHOUGH James's literary commitments are anchored in social and psychological realism and Emerson, in contrast, is essentially a mystic, Emerson's image of the self as a transparent eyeball provides a clarifying context for James's work with the character of consciousness. Emerson's eyeball is an image of self-transcendence; the boundaries that are ordinarily felt to separate the self from the world, the "I," or eye, from what it sees, are dissolved when Emerson says, "I am nothing. I see all. The currents of the Universal Being circulate through me" (*Nature*, p. 10). The particular self is transcended by taking into itself the world outside of it. James created a group of characters whose distinctive feature is a similar ability to transcend the self. He pointed to this achievement, which came to fruition in *The Spoils of Poynton* in the character of Fleda Vetch, when he commented on the character of Rowland Mallet in *Roderick Hudson*: "What happened to him was above all to feel certain things happening to others, to Roderick, to Christina, to Mary Garland, to Mrs. Hudson, to the Cavaliere, to the Prince" (*Prefaces*, p. 16). When what happens to others is felt as happening to the self, social and psychological realities touch borders with the mystical. But James's characters transfer the ground of self-transcendence from nature, where Emerson located it, to society. Consciousness then takes into itself principally other people: not the natural landscape, but the social one. The ramifications of this change for the identity and autonomy of the self in James are enormous.

James's characters of consciousness live in a world made vivid by the social and psychological risks implicit in Emersonian Transcendentalism, though Emerson took care to defend consciousness from the consequences of those risks by situating it apart from society, in nature. Quentin Anderson, Richard Poirier, and Tony Tanner, who productively place Emerson at the center of America's literary tradition, present the problems of an American visionary self (Poirier locates it specifically in Emerson's eyeball image) that cannot adequately represent itself in or grapple with the social, material world.[1] Formulating the continuities between Emerson and James, they see James as having attempted to escape from the limitations of this world in his fiction by creating what Anderson calls an "imperial" or "hypertrophied" self, a character who through powers of imaginative expansion seeks to create another world, apart from this one.

The obstacles that threaten such expansiveness have typically been located in forces outside of the self. From Ezra Pound to Stephen Donadio, whose recent study of Nietzsche and James explores, among other things, their common debts to Emerson, the threat has been located in society, most devastatingly in "the pressures and encroachments of other wills."[2] Sallie Sears, formulating the matter in terms of competing authorial visions, proposes this melodramatic paradigm: the "imaginary worlds that the characters create for themselves annihilate each other. They cannot coexist because the victory of one *by definition* means the undoing of the other."[3] The same melodramatic formulation is offered by James himself when he contemplates "that bright hard medal, of so strange an alloy, one face of which is somebody's right and ease and the other somebody's pain and wrong" (*Prefaces*, p. 143).

Yet James also showed that, external forces aside, the self could be its own worst enemy. In an implicit critique of Emerson, he questioned whether a self that has transcended its particular identity can avoid losing itself. He suggests that the threat or restriction that finally matters most for consciousness comes from points of view and desires that have been incorporated into the self from outside of it and take possession of its center. As we have seen with Isabel Archer, James's characters of consciousness identify with certain points of view that they contain more compellingly than with any that might be considered their own. Such a process, in which the self evaporates instead of expanding, poisons the roots of artistry for these characters and subverts the concept of the "imperial self."

In grounding my presentation of Jamesian self-transcendence in Emerson, I am not so much trying to establish a line of direct influence, though Emerson was a living presence in both the James family household and the New England culture in which the Jameses grew up. Rather, Emerson is a valuable point of departure for this study because he gave the theme of visionary, or self-transcendent, possession of experience "life and flamboyance; it was he who generated it into [a] literary mythology," which made it available to other American writers "through agencies more mysterious than direct literary influence."[4]

For Emerson, then, in the famous epiphany of chapter 1 in *Nature*,

Standing on the bare ground,—my head bathed by the blithe air, and uplifted into infinite space,—all mean egotism vanishes. I become a transparent eye-ball. I am nothing. I see all. The currents of the Universal Being circulate through me;

I am part or particle of God. The name of the nearest friend sounds then foreign and accidental. To be brothers, to be acquaintances,—master or servant, is then a trifle and a disturbance. (P.10)

For Emerson, the self was primary, yet its status was precarious. In becoming universalized, the personal self or "mean ego" ceased to exist. Afloat in nature and one with it, an eyeball without a body, incorporeal and in an important sense anonymous, Emerson's image projects what might be called a self-less self.

Emerson conceived of himself as being all the more himself for being continuous with the world, all the more his particular self for being part of a universal identity. He was capable at times of making selfhood and otherness coincide with absolute success: "Spirit, that is, the Supreme Being, does not build up nature around us, but puts it forth through us, as the life of the tree puts forth new branches and leaves through the pores of the old" (*Nature*, p. 38).

Yet overall, there are serious difficulties for Emerson in believing that the particular self can find its essence and meaning through an epiphanic oneness with the universe. According to Roy Harvey Pearce, who brilliantly isolates this problem in American literature and culture, "Emerson's characteristic failures result from his striving so much to universalize the self that it gets lost in the striving."[5] Jonathan Bishop notes that Emerson's way of existing in community was to be there hardly at all, to have others "hear from me what I never spoke."[6] In addressing this paradox of selfless selfhood, however, Bishop tends to dissolve the tensions, as in his discussion of this journal entry: "All that we care for in a man is the tidings he gives us of our own faculty through the new conditions under which he exhibits the Common Soul."[7] Bishop's gloss is "We are, potentially, already in the only point of view from which the whole can be understood."[8]

While this is helpful on one level, on another it perpetuates the problem. If all that we care for in a man is what he tells us about ourselves and the universal soul, how can we know him? How can we have a relationship with him? Anderson comments that Emersonian consciousness "denies that our sense of ourselves is based on a reciprocal or dramatic or dialectic awareness of one another."[9] Yet to do away with other is to do dialectical damage to the self.

These difficulties can be summed up in the observation that Emerson lacked a social theory, a theory that could explain how the self is to keep the company of others (a lack that caused him pain and stumbling especially in "Experience"). At the end of the eyeball passage in *Nature*, all relations are disavowed. Friends, brothers, acquaintances, masters, and servants are all dismissed. The Emersonian self is universalized without being socialized. It does not know how to have a conversation or a relationship with another self even though— even perhaps because—self and other are conceived as one. James, however, made central in his work the question of how the self is to keep the company of others in a way that might preserve the integrity of both.

James consciously focused on the tenuousness of the Emersonian personal self in an ambivalent description of Emerson that comes rather close to characterizing his own characters of consciousness: "He had polished his aloofness till it reflected the image of his solicitor [that is, the person asking something of him]. And this was not because he was an 'uncommunicating egotist,' though he amuses himself with saying so to Miss Fuller: egotism is the strongest of passions, and he was altogether passionless. It was because he had no personal, just as he had almost no physical wants."[10] James's characters of consciousness also act as though they have "no personal . . . wants." And the imagery of mirrors and reflectors, used here to describe Emerson, James often employed in the prefaces to describe those characters. One implication of the image is the risk that identity may be constituted largely by what it mirrors, that the self may be defined by what is outside of it. This image of the self as a reflector, of consciousness as a mirror, receiving its identity from outside of itself, closely resembles and helps us to understand the stereotypical feminine self scrutinized by feminists. The image beautifully articulates the paradox that seems to define female identity—that women are more sensitive, more conscious than men, but that these assets often fail to give them an advantage. Because of them, in fact, women are generally less able to bring a personal self into existence.

Some of James's remarks about his mother evoke this image of a mirror-self, a selfless self: "She lived in ourselves so exclusively, with such a want of use for anything in her consciousness that was not about us and for us, that I think we almost contested her being separate enough to be proud of us—it was too like our being proud of ourselves." Even more pointedly: "She *was* he [the senior James, her husband], *was* each of us."[11] An expert at what one might call selfless or evacuated selfhood, Mrs. James makes real Poulet's image of the Jamesian fictional self as a decentered circle.

By saying the James character of consciousness is lacking a personal self in an important and revealing sense, however, I do not mean to imply that Strether, for example, does not feel a personal sort of pleasure from *dejeuner* with Madame de Vionnet, or that Fleda Vetch lacks a defining context of realistic detail, such as the possession of a father in West Kensington. Fleda may even manifest a perverse sort of self-gratification or egoism in her desire, while getting nothing for herself, to take charge of the affairs of others. Leon Edel sensitively discusses the way Mrs. James could be self-sacrificial, and yet "all-encompassing," even " 'gubernatorial.' "[12] What I mean by saying that the James character of consciousness lacks a personal self, then, is that in terms of the novels' psychic flow, the energies of Fleda and Strether's egos are severely disrupted. Though they are personages in their books, Fleda and Strether are also empty centers much of the time. They accumulate experience, but lack what would be thought of as a self.

In creating characters of consciousness like Fleda Vetch and Strether, James in effect socialized or domesticated Emerson's visionary eyeball self. Being visionary now meant floating out over other characters' consciousness, becoming a medium of reception capable of registering what it was like to be them, at the risk, as with Emerson, of making the personal self tenuous. It is precisely here, where the social and the mystical overlap (in mysticism, the self feels that it is in communion with a reality larger than itself), that James touches Emerson. In his 1918 memorial essay, which is still one of the most fertile sources of ideas about James, T. S. Eliot maintained that "The real hero, in any of James's stories, is a social entity of which men and women are constituents. . . . Compared with James's, other novelists' characters seem to be only accidentally in the same book."[13] Eliot was commenting on the profoundly social nature of James's work, but social in this case means that the work shows a concern with the fabric of awareness that constitutes communities of intimacy. On the whole, in James, these communities are woven from the narrative center outward as that character makes a relation with other characters by registering their desires and points of view.

James invokes these ideas about the self in relation to others in the preface to *The Spoils of Poynton* when he calls Fleda Vetch a "free spirit." He means by that term something close to an Emersonian eyeball self. The "free spirit," James says, "almost demonically both sees and feels, while the others [the "fools," who are "the fixed constituents" of the action] but feel without seeing" (*Prefaces*, p. 129). The others are fixed in the sense that they are trapped inside of themselves by the very intensity of their feelings, in what might be called the tyrannous centricity of the self, with all of its purely personal desires and claims. It was probably in order to get free of this narrow conception of personality posed by an exclusively self-centric way of being in the world that James invented the novelistic version of transcendental consciousness we know as the James character of consciousness, or the "free spirit." Fleda is free by virtue of the fact that she can see what is outside of herself; she can get beyond herself.

James valued empathic imagining so highly because he equated it with morality. He wrote of "the perfect dependence of the 'moral' sense of a work of art on the amount of felt life concerned in producing it" (*Prefaces*, p. 45), and implied the perfect dependence of a moral sense in people, or in characters that represent people, on the "amount of felt life" they can feel. To get outside of the self and imagine what experience feels like to others is to experience greater and greater amounts of "felt life" oneself. This conception of morality also, I believe, helps to explain James's preference for the technique of the central consciousness over the technique of first-person narration. In the preface to *The Ambassadors*, James speaks disenchantedly of "the terrible *fluidity* of self-revelation" (*Prefaces*, p. 321). The phrase suggests that he viewed first-person narration as inundatingly self-centric, a way of being in the world in which the self floods out all others.

The question provoked by James's comments on the free spirit is whether a commitment to what is ordinarily thought of as the personal self, or personality, need spell the death of freedom. Is it really liberating to be a self without a center? In dissolving the separation between self and other, and getting beyond the fixed limits ordinarily imposed by a sense of self, the free spirit makes a kind of contact with other selves that the Emerson persona customarily cannot manage. Yet despite the virtually limitless possibilities for growth perhaps potentially sponsored by self-transcendence in a social setting, the totally decentered self in James constitutes an invitation to melodrama and repression. For when James's characters escape the potential tyranny of their own personalities by making consciousness an instrument for encompassing other characters' feelings, they are in danger of being occupied at their centers by these competitive versions of experience. In Poulet's terms, "the object of attention [the person being observed] becomes the point of arrival of a movement of prospection and exploration. . . . So everything changes, consciousness, from central, becoming peripheral, and the object contemplated, becoming the central objective."[14] The result, when the "object of attention" is another character, is that the imagination of the narrative center is given over to this now "central objective" and subdued to its desires and the compositions of reality prescribed by these desires. Usually these are compositions that cause the characters of consciousness to disclaim their own desires. Such renunciation is a logical result of self-transcendence, a predictable outcome for characters who regard their own emotions primarily as a form of limitation.

————————THE SPOILS OF POYNTON————————

In *The Spoils of Poynton* (1897), James turns his concern with the limits imposed on the imagination by decenteredness into a study of ambassadorial consciousness. The transcendental character of consciousness in James often appears on the social scene as an intermediary or ambassador. *The Ambassadors, In the Cage,* and even *What Maisie Knew* come to mind, in addition to *The Spoils of Poynton*. Ambassadors are persons empowered by others to realize goals and purposes not their own, or only adoptively theirs. Although they may have a measure of freedom to negotiate independently and may even enter, at times, into a kind of working partnership with the bargaining parties, they are still not negotiating for themselves. Even if their employer's purposes and emotions become their own, the spoils will finally go to other parties. Strether's renunciatory ideal at the end of *The Ambassadors*, " 'not, out of the whole affair, to have got anything for myself,' " is a kind of manifesto of ambassadorial service. The same ideal governs the labors of Fleda Vetch up until the critical point at which she allows herself, at Owen's invitation, to journey to Poynton to pick an object of personal gain from among the spoils.

Fleda, like Strether, is employed to conduct diplomacy between mother and son. Her life as an ambassador begins when she is pressed to undertake for the widowed Mrs. Gereth and her son Owen the touchy negotiations that have arisen over the possession of Poynton's contents as a result of Owen's upcoming and, as it turns out, contingent marriage to Mona Brigstock. Mrs. Gereth and her son "transmit through" Fleda; she is their "communicator" (10:83), their "envoy" (10:139), and virtually leaves herself out as she negotiates on their behalf. She identifies with their picture of her as an ambassador to such a degree that even when they want her to profit personally from the negotiations, she remains committed to ambassadorial consciousness.

The egoless, free-floating quality of the Emersonian eyeball is especially apparent when Owen offers to buy Fleda a token of appreciation for her assistance with his mother. Fleda busies herself "wondering what Mona would think of such proceedings." "What she noticed most was that . . . [Owen] said no word of his intended" (10:63, 64). When Fleda construes Owen's "unsounded words" as an offer to live with her at Ricks, she "could only vainly wonder how it provided for poor Mona" (10:101). And when she hears that Mona jealously suspects her motives in continuing to negotiate between Owen and his mother, "It was a sudden drop in her great flight, a shock to her attempt to watch over Mona's interests" (10:164–65). The conjunction here of imagery of flight and vision conjures up a flying eyeball, with, in this case, intentionally comic effect. The eyeball's unexpected "drop" is a pratfall that sub-

jects the enterprise it implicitly signifies—self-transcendence—
to intended scrutiny. (In *The Wings of the Dove*, Milly watches
over the interests of Densher and Kate Croy in a selfless flight
that is subjected to some of the same scrutiny.) Fleda's effort
to "watch over Mona's interests" extends the role of intermediary to which Owen and his mother first appointed her.
The fact that Mona has not employed her as an ambassador
makes even clearer her need to negotiate on behalf of someone else, on behalf of anyone except herself.

Robert C. McLean questions the self-transcending capacity
of Fleda's imagination, and contends that Fleda is imprisoned
in herself and that her imaginings of others should be taken
as delusions and self-projections.[15] Richard A. Hocks, however, insists that Fleda is genuinely self-transcendent:

> Her ethic is . . . pragmatistically oriented—that is, parallel to
> William's own broadening or "radical" aspects of utilitarian-
> ism—in that Fleda characteristically *creates* a possible other case
> about Mona, projects a version of the other girl as someone
> for whom Owen's earlier proposal is "a tremendous thing,"
> someone who "must" love him because Fleda herself does. The
> saltatory mind can immediately say that Fleda is merely cre-
> ating Mona in her own image, and that is so to the extent that
> she . . . makes Mona's feelings coalesce with her own. To the
> same saltatory mind that sounds simply like making others into
> yourself. In fact it is just the reverse: it is conceiving of each
> person as so distinctively individual that you are willing con-
> tinually to subsume your own views into them rather than clas-
> sify them as Other.[16]

When Fleda attributes feelings to Mona that cannot be verified, however, there is good reason to think that if she is not
creating Mona in her image, she is externalizing her own feelings by means of Mona. Fleda's displacement of her own
emotion onto Mona is particularly apparent when she argues

with Owen about Mona's reasons for postponing the wedding: " 'Doesn't it occur to you . . . that if Mona is, as you say, drawing away, she may have in doing so a very high motive? She knows the immense value of all the objects detained by your mother, and to restore the spoils of Poynton she's ready . . . to make a sacrifice. The sacrifice is that of an engagement she had entered upon with joy' " (10:160). With such reasoning, Fleda injects into Mona's motives her own high-tonedness, tenderness, and inclination to sacrifice. When Fleda greets the prospect of Owen's disengagement from Mona with the question, " 'Can you take such pleasure in her being "finished"—a poor girl you've once loved?' " (10:187), it is easier to recognize Fleda herself as the piteous " 'poor girl' " about to be " 'finished' " than it is to recognize the robust Mona. And when Fleda exhorts Owen not to " 'break faith' " with Mona because " 'She must love you—how can she help it? *I* wouldn't give you up! . . . Never, never, never!' " (10:196–97), she seems to be saying that Mona must love Owen because she, Fleda, does. Although she claims that she would not give Owen up, the irony, of course, is that she does so, as though she had quite emptied herself of these emotions in attributing them to Mona.

Fleda later imagines the suffering of Ricks' maiden aunt in a flight of consciousness that, like her imagination of Mona, is never verified. In contrast, we accept Maggie Verver's imagination of Charlotte's shriek and Amerigo's pacing as the unquestionable reality of *The Golden Bowl* because Maggie's self is sufficiently present to make what she imagines *become* novelistic reality. Fleda feels her own emotions best by giving them away, however, and as a result she responds to them in a self-defeating way. When she expresses her own love by imagining Mona's love for Owen, for instance, her interests are displaced in her consciousness by Mona's; and Mona's dictate that she, Fleda, shall renounce the young man. Thus

Fleda actively labors for this end, as though for some cause of her own.

Mrs. Gereth also serves as an external agent by which Fleda experiences her own emotional life. At first, Mrs. Gereth's disapproval of Mona as Owen's fiancée seems to express an oedipal competitiveness: removing the furnishings from Poynton looks like competing with Mona for them, and for Owen. But in the flow of raw psychic energy beneath the novel's surface, the mother's sexual dimension becomes Fleda's own in dislocation, giving form to Fleda's barely recognized stirrings. She encourages Fleda to compete with Mona on sexual terms: " 'I want you to cut in!' . . . She challenged again and again Fleda's picture, as she called it (though the sketch was too slight to deserve the name), of the indifference to which a prior attachment had committed the proprietor of Poynton. . . . 'Only let yourself go, darling—only let yourself go!' " (10:141–42). When Fleda returns from a trip to London, in the course of which she has lost track of Owen rather than letting herself go to him, and she tries to calm Mrs. Gereth while submitting to her interrogation, Mrs. Gereth "rose again from where Fleda had kept her down" (10:218), like Fleda's own impulses. Mrs. Gereth's lecture "affected our young lady as if it had been the shake of a tambourine borne toward her from a gipsy dance; her head seemed to go round and she felt a sudden passion in her feet" (10:220).

Thus inspired, Fleda sees the situation and herself with Mrs. Gereth's eyes, and consents, in James's metaphor, to dance to her patron's tambourine, with the result that her determination "to lose herself"—as James puts it when she hides from Owen in her father's West Kensington flat (10:144)—to claim nothing for herself, is for a moment suspended. She temporarily recomposes her sketch of the plot by volunteering to find Owen and marry him without further ado. She takes the extraordinary step, for her, of sending Owen a telegram asking him to come to her, putting her desire for him, until now displaced onto Mrs. Gereth and Mona, into words explicitly from her, hoping thus to disprove Mrs. Gereth's contention that she " 'could invent nothing better' " (10:223) than to send Owen back to Mona (Fleda's instructions to Owen in London). As a sign of her effort to concentrate her distributed energies into a personal self, Fleda even refuses Mrs. Gereth's offer to pay for the telegram: " 'To succeed it must be all me!' " (10:227).

Yet the incompleteness of her effort to locate a self—to " 'be all me' "—and to recompose the sketch is evident even as she awaits an answer to the telegram. James evokes her psychic division in terms of a virtually Freudian architecture. "Her trouble occupied some quarter of her soul that had closed its doors for the day and shut out even her own sense of it; she might perhaps have heard something if she had pressed her ear to a partition. Instead of that she sat with her patience in a cold still chamber from which she could look out in quite another direction" (10:234). Absent from the scene of her trouble, she remains partitioned off from her own emotional life. She sits in less private spaces of the self, unable to inhabit the full residence. Thus when Mrs. Gereth brings her the news that Owen is already married, "All the girl's effort tended for the time to a single aim—that of taking the thing with outward detachment, speaking of it as having happened to Owen and to his mother and not in any degree to herself" (10:237–38).

Fleda's way of owning pain is, as it was before, with other emotions, to register it in another self. With Owen married, Fleda prepares for a life of memories and spinsterhood, enhanced in her eyes by qualities she attributes to Ricks' former proprietor, a maiden aunt. From the beginning, her unverified imagination of the aunt's life contains her own feelings of suffering: "The poor lady . . . had been sensitive and ignorant and exquisite. . . . [Fleda] was so sure she had deeply suffered" (10:54–55). On her third visit to Ricks, after Mrs. Gereth has sent back the furnishings stolen from Poynton and reinstated the maiden aunt's few effects, Fleda hears these speak with a voice full of her own sense of frailness: " 'a voice so gentle, so human, so feminine—a faint far-away voice with the little quaver of a heart-break.' " It is a voice that turns deprivation into something romantic and appealing, something "exquisite." Fleda has the sense of " 'something dreamed and missed, something reduced, relinquished, resigned: the poetry, as it were, of something sensibly *gone*' " (10:249). In deriving poetic pleasure from this contemplation, Fleda can aestheticize such suffering as might well be her own and, in doing so, avoid the acknowledgment of her own pain that might enable her to throw it off.

Even at this late date, she chooses to remain "vague" about the nature of her pain:

> Then Fleda said: "What I mean is, for this dear one of ours [the aunt], that if she had (as I *know* she did: it's in the very touch of the air!) a great accepted pain—"
> She had paused an instant, and Mrs. Gereth took her up. "Well, if she had?"
> Fleda still hung fire. "Why, it was worse than yours."
> Mrs. Gereth debated. "Very likely." Then she too hestitated. "The question is if it was worse than yours."
> "Mine?" Fleda looked vague. (10:250)

Though her consciousness does not register the pain as her own, Fleda herself has become part of the spoilage of Poynton.

Although Fleda has been employed by Owen and his mother, she betrays them both, promoting events that probably neither of them wants to occur. Mona, who never appointed Fleda, is, ironically, the one party whose interests she does not betray. No sooner does she sense that Owen might want her to help him end his engagement, and that she herself might want to help, than she fosters a sequence of events leading to the return of the spoils to Poynton, a move she knows will satisfy Mona and precipitate the marriage. Mona is the character from whose point of view Fleda essentially operates—Mona and perhaps the maiden aunt. As a character of consciousness, incorporating other selves at the expense of her own sense of self, Fleda necessarily favors characters whose pictures or fictions of experience commit her to strategies of personal loss.

Skepticism about Fleda's renunciation is fed by what seems to be a desire on her part for visible justification and moral simplification. Before the marriage, when Owen seeks Fleda out at her sister's, he hears, " 'Ah you see it's not true that you're free!' She seemed almost to exult. 'It's not true—it's not true' " (10:196): a crow of satisfaction rather than, as one might expect, a lament. To Mrs. Gereth's news that Owen is married Fleda responds, " 'That he has done it, that he couldn't *not* do it, shows how right I was' " (10:239). Subsequently her certainty about what is right seduces her into a dead language, a rhetoric suggesting that what she embraces as rightness may be rigidity. When Owen invites her, after his marriage, to take something from him, something from Poynton, the best thing in the collection, or whatever she most loves, she feels compelled to reason out the invitation, straining all the way, as "a token of gratitude for having kept him in the straight path" (10:260). To a reader, this rhetorical deadness undermines her renunciatory selflessness as much as it undermines Isabel's when Isabel turns, rhetorically and literally, to the rigid rightness of the "straight path" to show her what to do after the confusion of Caspar's kiss.

The tenuousness of Fleda's personal self, her tendency to turn to Mona or the maiden aunt for tidings of her own condition, prevents her from achieving full authorial status in the book and, therefore, from making the prevailing picture

of the plot accommodate her own desires. The implications
for authorship of Fleda's renunciatory consciousness can be
seen best by returning to the figure of Mrs. Gereth. James
calls her "the very reverse of a free spirit" (*Prefaces*, p. 131).
"She had no imagination about anybody's life save on the side
she bumped against. . . . Mrs. Gereth had really no perception
of anybody's nature—had only one question about persons:
were they clever or stupid?" (10:138)—were they, that is, capable of appreciating Poynton? Imprisoned in her narrowly
defined particular self, Mrs. Gereth is, in Emersonian terms,
a "mean egotist." She lacks the largeness of vision to appre-
hend others on their own terms—and thus to be a figure of
consciousness. For example, when she moves from Poynton
to the dowerhouse, redecorating it with furnishings stolen
from Poynton, she is at first so devoid of empathic imaginative
response to the meager but touching objects left by her pred--
ecessor that, Fleda feels, "The maiden-aunt had been exter-
minated" (10:79). Nevertheless, once Mrs. Gereth returns the
spoils to Poynton, she reinstates the old aunt's few effects at
Ricks and makes them grow "indescribably sweet" (10:258)
around her. And despite her incomprehension of Fleda's nature and motives for betraying her, she keeps Fleda with her
at the end and cannot help but care for her, even if waspishly.

Mrs. Gereth is thus a complex figure in the allegiances the
novel creates in the reader. Even her devotion to the "mean
ego," the particular self, generates ambivalence. That James
intended this is suggested by the fact that her advice to Fleda
to let herself go echoes James's most urgent and moving ex-
hortation to himself in his notebooks, the record he kept of
his work in progress for more than thirty years. "I have only
to let myself *go*! So I have said to myself all my life. . . . Yet
I have never fully done it. The sense of it—of the need of
it—rolls over me. . . . I am in full possession of accumulated
resources—I have only to use them. . . . All life is—at my age,

with all one's artistic soul the record of it—in one's pocket, as it were. Go on, my boy, and strike hard: have a rich and long St. Martin's Summer" (*Notebooks*, p. 106).

Here in 1891 James speaks of his art in terms of the energies of Victorian commerce and, implicitly, its ethos of self-fulfillment: "accumulated resources" in "one's pocket" which it is imperative to "use." Composition is analogized not so much to saving (though there is talk in the prefaces about the economy of art) or to paying (which often takes the form in James of punishment and loss), but to having and spending, a difference of emphasis that suggests a generous regard for the resources of the self. Fleda's "imagination of a disaster" (10:262) as she travels down to Poynton to claim her gift is an aspect of James's own melodramatic vision, as James confessed to A. C. Benson the year before he published *The Spoils*: "I have the imagination of disaster—and see life indeed as ferocious and sinister."[17] Nevertheless, the letting go, which in the notebooks James required of himself for the sake of his art, is allied with the kinds of letting go—both emotional and sexual—by means of which Fleda herself could become authorial and purge the plot of *The Spoils* of its similarities to a genteelly-suffering-maiden-aunt melodrama. The invitation Mrs. Gereth extends to Fleda to let herself go and imagine herself beyond renunciation is, in effect, James's own.

Although Emerson opposed the values of the genteel tradition, particularly the failure of originality in its indebtedness to the European inheritance, and although he periodically, in his essays, issued calls to action in the material world, his image of the self as an incorporeal eyeball floating cleanly above a world of getting and spending has something in common with the disengagement from experience prized by the genteel tradition. This attitude characterizes the genteel tradition even though it reached its vantage of disengagement from a base of compromising material security. In electing to work with the character of consciousness, James departed from both Emerson and the genteel tradition. He showed that to be free of worldly and personal desires, nevertheless, is not to be free—that for the earthbound, integrity and a measure of freedom necessarily come through the personal self and the satisfaction of earthly desires. Although Fleda resists the invitation, the pressures of James's material point toward the possibility of a consciousness capable both of possessing itself without becoming self-absorbed and possessing its world instead of losing itself in it.

James wished to evaluate the costs of being a transparent eyeball lodged in a material world. The costs for Fleda are an inability to include much of her world in her composition of it. For example, though Fleda has rendered a sense of Owen's love through her consciousness, she does not know his pain; there is no space for that in the novel as her awareness composes it. The destruction of Poynton and its contents by fire is the ultimate symbol of Fleda's authorial failure, the result and the sign of her inability to imagine for herself an existence and a plot that could incorporate what the spoils in the largest sense include: love, sexuality, and ownership in the physical, material world.[18] The novel suggests that Poynton burns because Fleda's sketch of experience affords no space to those desires of the particular self. To save it would require a self capable of being both eyeball and body.[19]

James creates the impression in several ways that the destruction of Poynton is both symbol and consequence of Fleda's absence from herself and the design she has promoted. It is partly a matter of timing. The house goes up in flames on the precise morning Fleda has picked, after weeks of waiting, for her visit to claim the gift Owen has invited her to take. The accusatory effect is heightened by an eerie sense that the objects of Poynton have suddenly come to life to take revenge on Fleda for abandoning them to Mona's negligent hands. A sense of dislocated energy further relates the fire to Fleda's selflessness: it is as if her desire at last to get something for herself triggers in her a fantasy of guilt and punishment which is projected onto the external world in the destruction of what she loves.

An author in James must ultimately participate in and profit from the design in order to be assured of "*supreme* command" over the fictional arrangements. In Maggie Verver, James did create a character of consciousness capable both of transcending the self and fully occupying its center, being both other and self, eyeball and body, a fusion that enables her to be a fully successful artist of her situation. But Fleda is unable to make the spoils (the objects and the book) her *Spoils* in the way that Osmond can make Isabel his *Portrait* and Maggie can make the bowl (object and book) her *Bowl*. The *Spoils* resembles *The Wings of the Dove* in that imagination and consciousness acquire a certain degree of control over the plot, but not enough to secure the predominance of their designs. In *The Wings of the Dove*, Milly seeks to compose shapes for the lives around her through her will, the "sacred script" (20:386) she leaves behind after her death, but in her absence she cannot make the design take hold. Presiding authorially from a distance proves to be an inadequate sort of authorship for Strether too when, in lecturing Chad at the end of *The Ambassadors*, he futilely delegates to the young man his own desire to love and protect Madame de Vionnet.

THE AMBASSADORS

In *The Ambassadors* (1903), James continued to explore the connections between consciousness, selfhood, and authorship by developing even further than he had in *The Spoils* the metaphor of ambassadorial mission. Through the metaphor of the ambassador, the novel encompasses a study of substitutive or second-hand agency, a type of unoriginal relation to the world in which Strether's absence from himself inevitably traps him. In the first of many substitutions which he either co-operates with or initiates, Strether agrees at the beginning of the novel to replace Mrs. Newsome. To Waymarsh, the American friend he joins in Europe, he explains " 'I've come in a manner instead of her' " (21:32)—to negotiate with her son Chad on her behalf. He is appointed only to represent Mrs. Newsome's interest, not to develop his own relationship with Chad, Paris, or the woman Mrs. Newsome is sure holds Chad in her clutches. Maria Gostrey, an expatriate American and Strether's guide to the experience of Europe, discerns regarding his relationship with Mrs. Newsome that " 'The way it works—you needn't tell me!—is of course that you efface yourself' " (21:65). And he volunteers to Miss Barrace, a friend of Chad, that he has no " 'life of my own . . . not for myself. I seem to have a life only for other people' " (21:269).

Complaining to Waymarsh of the indeterminate, ambiguous appearances which are the substance of European experience, Strether is moved to assert a personal, independent purpose potentially at odds with self-effacement and ambassadorial employment—" 'to see for myself' " (21:109). He does not yet know anything definite about Chad's putative depravity, the lurid version of her son's prolonged stay in Paris with which Mrs. Newsome has sent him over, but he begins to find a plea-sure in the possibility of a different version that he may de-termine for himself; that pleasure begins, quite simply, with his acceptance of not knowing: " 'Well, ' said Strether almost gaily, 'I guess I don't know anything!' His gaiety might have been a tribute to the fact that the state he had been reduced to . . . was somehow enlarging" (21:106).

When Strether feels sure that he knows what is keeping Chad in Paris, his language reflects the imprisoning simpli-fication of a sexual melodrama. Maria Gostrey is the first to challenge the simplifications about sexuality in which Streth-er's imagination has trapped him: " 'What else but such a somebody can such a miracle [Chad's apparent improvement] be? . . . *A* woman. Some woman or other. It's one of the things that *have* to be.' 'But you mean then at least a good one.' 'A good woman?' She threw up her arms with a laugh. 'I should call her excellent!' " (21:169–70). Maria tries to get Strether to reconsider the reductive premise behind his words: the assumption that women can be divided into good and bad, and that the difference between them is that a bad woman is sexual, while a good woman, by definition, is not.

Strether turns also to little Bilham and to Chad himself for rhetoric by which to simplify his understanding of the young man's relation with Madame de Vionnet. Little Bilham suggests for the relation the large and conveniently ambiguous term "virtuous attachment" (21:180). Chad proposes the conundrum a "life without reproach":

> "Excuse me, but I must really . . . know where I am. Is she bad?" [Strether asks.]
>
> " 'Bad'?"—Chad echoed it, but without a shock. "Is that what's implied—?"
>
> "When relations are good?" Strether felt a little silly. . . . He none the less at last found something. "Is her life without reproach?"
>
> It struck him, directly he had found it, as pompous and priggish; so much so that he was thankful to Chad for taking it only in the right spirit. . . . "Absolutely without reproach. A beautiful life." (21:239)

Through verbal puzzles or conundra, among the most sophisticatedly indefinite of the arts of conversation, Maria Gostrey, little Bilham, and Chad teach Strether to postpone his need for fixed knowledge (" 'I must really . . . know where I am' "). Evading him without precisely lying to him, they put forward a form of truth that Strether has later to acknowledge is only a "technical lie" (22:299).

To put it another way, artful, even deceptive, speech and

manners may enlarge the possibilities of the real and the right.
The Ambassadors thus represents a further stage of reconciliation of the dialectic in James between style and substance,
artfulness and trustworthiness, surface and depth, which
reaches its fullest synthesis in Maggie Verver of *The Golden
Bowl*. The controlling image of this dialectic in *The Ambassadors*
is the jewel that Paris, in all of its stylish complexity, strikes
Strether as being. Its many facets make it a conundrum in
the realm of the physically decorative, for with its twinkling,
"what seemed all surface one moment seemed all depth the
next" (21:89). Thus Madame de Vionnet's genius, as Strether
realizes when he discovers her subterfuge at the end of the
book, resides in making artifice and naturalness coincide. She
represents the place where surface and depth meet, and it is
fruitless to distinguish between them.

> She had never, with him, been more . . . [natural and simple];
> or if it was the perfection of art it would never—and that came
> to the same thing—be proved against her.
> What was truly wonderful was her way of differing so from
> time to time without detriment to her simplicity. . . . once more
> and yet once more, he could trust her. That is he could trust
> her to make deception right. (22:276–77)

These astounding discriminations about human behavior
suggest that although in Chad's case civilization may be a ve-
neer, in the case of Madame de Vionnet, and at its best, it
may be the enabling condition of our essential humanity.

The preponderance of superlatives in the late work is perhaps the technically purest evidence of James's interest in
making artfulness reveal and enhance essence. The superlatives are intensifiers; they appear obfuscatory, and yet their
mannered vagueness heightens reality. To Miss Barrace's
mind, for example, Waymarsh is " 'wonderful. . . . He doesn't
understand—not one little scrap. He's delightful. He's won-

derful' " (21:205). Readers who are acquainted by this time with Waymarsh may well do an auditory double take. Certainly there is the sense of a put-on here. But more important is the insight that Waymarsh *is* wonderful. Miss Barrace's stylistic flourish is intended to express admiration that Waymarsh is what he is (here, uncomprehending) with an intensity and totality to which no particularizing description could do justice.

Yet Strether, though he learns from and even masters this new way of talking, remains tied to his old self, still only Strether, almost as much as Chad is finally seen to be "none the less only Chad" (22:284). The extent of his disavowal of the moralistic and melodramatic imagination of Woollett frets naggingly at the text. Like *The Portrait*, this book carries much of its weight in its protagonist's sense of his capacity for growth and change, and in *our* sense of how fully he realizes this capacity. Strether's receptivity to new ways of thinking and also the limits of this receptivity emerge powerfully in the "Live all you can" speech he delivers to little Bilham, though the speech is often mistakenly understood solely as an indication of growth on Strether's part.

> "Live all you can; it's a mistake not to. . . . I'm old. . . . It's too late. . . . The affair—I mean the affair of life—couldn't, no doubt, have been different for me; for it's at the best a tin mould, either fluted and embossed, with ornamental excrescences, or else smooth and dreadfully plain, into which, a helpless jelly, one's consciousness is poured—so that one 'takes' the form, as the great cook says, and is more or less compactly held by it. . . . Still, one has the illusion of freedom; therefore don't be, like me, without the memory of that illusion. . . . The right time is *any* time that one is still so lucky as to have. . . . Do what you like so long as you don't make *my* mistake. . . . Live!" (21:217–18)

The advice that Strether gives—"Live all you can"—is hardly the advice that Woollett dispenses; it is, in fact, much closer to the European attitude toward experience. Yet the frozen view of character which Strether's image of the mold represents accords well with Woollett's inflexible posture in the face of new experience. The speech is aimed at inspiring little Bilham to live, rather than expressing some sense that Strether may change enough to do so. It is a part of Strether's substitutive approach to experience, not an alternative to it. Furthermore, the manner in which Strether delivers his message retains the didacticism and preachiness of the Woollett sensibility. The speech is a monologue, a sermon, rather than a reciprocal conversation of the kind through which Maria, little Bilham, and Chad have worked their instruction of Strether. Strether exhorts little Bilham, lectures him on his duty, contrives to turn experience into a lesson. It is for this reason that James intrudes with a wry qualification: "Slowly and sociably, with full pauses and straight dashes, Strether had so delivered himself. . . . The end of all was that the young man had turned quite solemn" (21:218).

Most of James's characters who make up for lost experience only indirectly—whether substitutively through others, or in memory, or in an elaborate life of consciousness in the present—are young. Thus it often becomes too late rather early in James. The "too late" theme—too late to change, to recover what has been lost, or to claim something new—is given more credibility in this novel than it is elsewhere in James by the fact that Strether, next to Isabel or Fleda, *is* comparatively old. And yet James undercuts Strether's argument that it is too late for him by making the image of the mold, which Strether employs as a symbol for determinism, backfire, in much the same way that the language from *Paradise Lost* backfires on Caspar in *The Portrait*.

Strether's way of speaking about the mold implies that one's life and character are fixed virtually from the beginning: consciousness " 'takes' the form . . . and is more or less compactly held." But James's manipulation of the image, as Gordon O. Taylor, among others, has noted, [20] calls this fixity into question. Thus, when Strether says that it is " 'the affair of life' " that provides the mold for consciousness and character, he is, in effect, removing from the metaphor of the mold the very static quality for which he evidently chose it. There is a reciprocal relation between life and character implicit in the language he has selected.

For if it is the whole affair of life that molds character, then it follows, since life is hardly a monolithic affair, that the addition of each new circumstance reshapes the mold and in turn broadens the range of experience by which character may be influenced. In Paris, for example, Strether receives many new impressions and, in turn, becomes capable of new appreciations, with the potential result that the very nature of the affair of life may in time change quite radically for him. The metaphor of the mold thus actually suggests that mistakes need not determine or deform the shape of an entire lifetime. Strether's admonition to little Bilham that " 'The right time is *any* time that one is still so lucky as to have' " seems potentially just as applicable to himself. In the formulation "the affair of life," James offered Strether a way to fulfill a possibility implicit in perhaps the best-known quotation from his seminal 1884 essay "The Art of Fiction." There James proposed: "If experience consists of impressions, it may be said that impressions *are* experience."[21] This suggests not only that reality is internal, and unique to each of us, but also that because the mind makes what we know as experience, we have a chance, by permitting ourselves to form new impressions, to have new experiences.

During the time that Strether tries to confront experience in a new, less rigidly knowing way, the memorable scene occurs on the river after which he divines that Chad and Madame de Vionnet are lovers. Holland maintains that after Strether's first meeting with Chad, when his imagination is revealed to be clearly inadequate to the complexities of the young man's relationship with the French woman, "the touches of melodrama in his imagination are vestigial."[22] But in the night-

long vigil after Strether finds the couple in the Parisian countryside, when he reads their intimacy in Madame de Vionnet's
unprecedented and evasive reliance on French as they dine,
and in the unfurnished casualness of her attire, he finally recognizes that if he thought he had progressed to the point of
not caring whether the couple's relation was good or bad, he
may nevertheless not have been prepared for the possibility
that their goodness might include sexuality. "His theory, as
we know, had bountifully been that the facts were specifically
none of his business, and were, over and above, so far as one
had to do with them, intrinsically beautiful; and this might
have prepared him for anything, as well as rendered him
proof against mystification. When he reached home that night,
however, he knew he had been, at bottom, neither prepared
nor proof" (22:261–62). James depicts Strether's difficulty in
making the transition from the enlarging provisional state of
knowing nothing definite to a state of finding what there is
to know also large, by transforming the scene from a composition in the style of the Barbizon school of French painting
to a canvas in the style of the Impressionists, who succeeded
them.

At first, the painting that the countryside specifically calls
up in Strether's mind is a French landscape by Lambinet.
Stepping down from the train, he finds that "The poplars
and willows, the reeds and river . . . fell into a composition.
. . . the sky was silver and turquoise and varnish; the village
on the left was white and the church on the right was grey.
. . . It was Tremont Street, it was France, it was Lambinet"
(22:247).[23] The scene soon, however, becomes an Impressionist canvas in his eyes. The trees and reeds, the sky, and
the village now "affected him as a thing of whiteness, blueness
and crookedness, set in coppery green" (22:252). Viola Hopkins Winner comments that this second description of the
scene offers a verbal equivalent for the painterly effects of the
Impressionists as "adjectives are converted into substan-

tives, a grammatical shift which places the emphasis on the sensory quality of the visual experience rather than on the thing itself."[24] To emphasize the sensory quality of the visual experience is to be hospitable to the way the experience changes with the season and the time of day. For the Impressionists, as for James when he speaks about "the affair of life," change, not fixity, is the truth about reality.

As Chad and Madame de Vionnet drift into view on the river,

> What . . . [Strether] saw was exactly the right thing—a boat advancing round the bend and containing a man who held the paddles and a lady, at the stern, with a pink parasol. . . . [They were] a young man in shirt-sleeves, a young woman easy and fair. . . . The air quite thickened, at their approach, with further intimations; the intimation that they were expert, familiar, frequent—that this wouldn't at all events be the first time. They knew how to do it, he vaguely felt. (22:256)

The shift from Barbizon to Impressionist art is a shift from an austere work ethos—peasant men and women laboring in the countryside—to an emphasis on romance and recreation—casual shirt-sleeves and a pink parasol. Chad and Madame de Vionnet are city dwellers on vacation in the countryside around Paris, a typical Impressionist subject.

The Lambinet in whose terms Strether first sees the countryside is a painting he passed up the chance to buy in a Boston art shop long ago when he felt he could not afford it. Because of the intimacy with which the addition of lovers on holiday infuses the scene, Strether still feels he cannot "afford" it. The switch in painting periods is intended to show that Strether's inability to possess the Lambinet in his youth is now compounded, not amended. His reluctance to "buy" the scene, once he arrives home and grasps its implications, prefigures his inability, ultimately, to change enough to lay claim to the material of his life and the novel. James shows why Strether's change has not been greater by focusing on his relationships with women.

Strether's change in Europe is largely due to and manifested in a new receptivity to women, even though it is precisely here that the limits of his change are most apparent. The women offered to his vision—Mrs. Newsome, Maria Gostrey, and Madame de Vionnet, with Jeanne de Vionnet, Mamie Pocock, and Sarah Pocock as more minor occasions for appreciation—constitute the main focal points of the story. Finding the young Mamie on the hotel balcony, for instance, Strether reflects that "his experience of remarkable women—destined, it would seem, remarkably to grow—felt itself ready this afternoon, quite braced itself, to include her" (22:148). In the scenario, James is explicit about the importance that Strether's relationships with women will have in the completed novel: "I don't want to represent every woman in the book beginning with Mrs. Newsome, as having, of herself, 'made up' to my hero. . . . But it's none the less a fact that Mrs. Newsome, Miss Gostrey, and poor magnificent Mme de Vionnet herself (though this last is a secret of secrets) have been, in the degree involved, agreeably and favourably affected by him" (*Notebooks*, p. 414).

Despite the fact that Strether is a "man marked out by women," as he puts it to himself about Chad, his response to sexuality resembles that of an uninitiated young man still under the maternal wing. When he first meets Chad, for instance, he is nonplussed not least by his apprehension of Chad's sexual presence: "He saw him in a flash as the young man marked out by women; and for a concentrated minute the dignity, the comparative austerity, as he funnily fancied it, of this character affected him almost with awe. . . . That was then the way men marked out by women *were*" (21:153–54). And when Strether reflects on the vision of the "deep, deep truth of the intimacy revealed" by the way in which Chad and Madame de Vionnet communicate with each other when he catches them in the Parisian suburbs, it is, again, with an emphasis so uninitiatedly awed that it verges on dread: "That was what, in his vain vigil, he oftenest reverted to: intimacy, at such a point, was *like* that—and what in the world else would one have wished it to be like?" (22:266).

Strether's experience at dinner and the theater with Maria Gostrey at the beginning of the book appears to count as virtually his first intimate experience with a woman, despite a wife and son in the early years of life, and his fiancée, Mrs. Newsome, in Boston:

> He had been to the theatre, even to the opera, in Boston, with Mrs. Newsome, more than once acting as her only escort; but there had been no little confronted dinner, no pink lights, no whiff of vague sweetness, as a preliminary. . . . There was much the same difference in his impression of the noticed state of his companion, whose dress was "cut down," as he believed the term to be, in respect to shoulders and bosom, in a manner quite other than Mrs. Newsome's. (21:50)

As Strether more and more makes his own way in Paris, however, Maria's friendship loses its romance:

> He could toddle alone. . . . The time seemed already far off when he had held out his small thirsty cup to the spout of her pail. Her pail was scarce touched now, and other fountains had flowed for him; she fell into her place as but one of his tributaries. . . .
> . . . It . . . [was] but the day before yesterday that he sat at her feet and held on by her garment and was fed by her hand.
> (22:48, 49)

Retrospectively, Strether sees himself in his early relation with Maria as an infant at the maternal source: holding on to the hem of her skirt, being fed from metaphoric pails and fountains. But he has matured enough to "toddle alone" now, and away from her. Even the offer of marriage which she manages to convey to Strether at the end of the novel he sees as an "offer of exquisite service, of lightened care, for the rest of his days" (22:325–26), traditionally, maternal offices. Maria has launched him—as Ralph launched Isabel in *The Portrait*—beyond her. Her parental power has taken the benign form of making him grow independent of her.

Yet though he can "place" Maria "as but one of his tributaries," and grow beyond her, he cannot "place" the more ominously maternal Mrs. Newsome who, in her invisible omnipresence, continues to brood over his life. James worried about the degree of success he had had in rendering Mrs. Newsome's omnipresence, and it is obvious he meant that to be one of the novel's most important effects:

> Such an element, for instance, as . . . [the author's] intention that Mrs. Newsome, away off with her finger on the pulse of Massachusetts, should yet be no less intensely than circuitously present through the whole thing, should be no less felt as to be reckoned with than the most direct exhibition . . . could make her, such a sign of artistic good faith, I say, once it's unmistakeably [*sic*] there, takes on again an actuality not too much impaired by the comparative dimness of the particular success. (*Prefaces*, p. 319)

At the heart of *The Ambassadors* is Strether's relationship with Mrs. Newsome, despite the fact that she never appears.

Though the purpose of Strether's ambassadorial mission is to bring home Chad, the real son, the circumstances of the mission make it a test of filial obedience for Strether himself in relation to Mrs. Newsome. Writing Mrs. Newsome nightly letters or reports of his performance, he realizes that "she wouldn't write [back to him] till Sarah should have seen him and reported on him" (22:47). He discovers from Jim Pocock that Mrs. Newsome is so concerned about his progress that she is metaphorically " 'sitting up' " for him " 'all night' " (22:89), like an anxious mother for a wayward child. And he falls to wondering if he may not be "disinherited beyond appeal" (22:144), like a bad child, for failing to bring Chad home. (Chad, of course, runs this very risk if he does not return.) The disinheritance to which he refers is the possibility that Mrs. Newsome may refuse to continue subsidizing the Woollett journal of which he is editor, and that she may refuse to marry him. She has made the marriage the implicit reward for succeeding with her ambassadorial errand. But even his picture of married life with Mrs. Newsome, like his picture of married life with Maria Gostrey, is filled with the rest and safety of maternal offices: " 'Well, at your age, and with what—when all's said and done—Mother might do for you and be for you' [Chad volunteers]. . . . Strether after an instant himself took a hand. 'My absence of an assured future. The little I have to show toward the power to take care of myself. The way, the wonderful way, she would certainly take care of me' " (22:238).

Maria Gostrey puts Strether in the position of showing that he falls in very substantially with Mrs. Newsome's maternal vision of their relationship: " 'Do you want Mrs. Newsome—after such a way of treating you?' . . . 'I dare say it has been, after all, the only way she could have imagined.' 'And does that make you want her any more?' [Marie queried.] 'I've tremendously disappointed her,' Strether thought it worth while [sic] to mention" (22:216). Strether cooperates, in this exchange, with Mrs. Newsome's imagination of him by focusing on his having, like a little boy, " 'disappointed' " her. He never answers the questions Maria asks about whether he still wants Mrs. Newsome after the way she has treated him, questions that would require him to think of the way he feels as well as of the way Mrs. Newsome feels.

Watching over Mrs. Newsome's interests and feelings, as

Fleda watches over Mona's, Strether overlooks his own feelings, not least his feelings *about* Mrs. Newsome. In the scenario, James sensed the possibility of a falling off in precisely this area, just as he had sensed a failing in his presentation of Claire de Cintré's psychological development in *The American*: "Reading these pages over, for instance, I find I haven't at all placed in a light what I make of the nature of Strether's feelings—his affianced, indebted, and other, consciousness—about Mrs. Newsome" (*Notebooks*, p. 415). It is the precise relation of Strether's sense of having disappointed Mrs. Newsome to his determination to return to Woollett that is most dimly lit in the book, although it can even perhaps be argued that the absence of this psychological connective tissue is one of the more important ways in which the book conveys its picture of Strether's suppressed development.

Strether's feelings about Mrs. Newsome exist in a space made silent by them both. He treats the subject of her with an almost superstitious hesitation, and mostly meets Maria's inquiries with the wail, " 'Oh I can't talk of her!' " (21:63). Mrs. Newsome, for her part, conveys her anger and disappointment to Strether by withdrawing her dependably frequent correspondence, although her silence makes her no less present to him:

> He had for some time been aware that he was hearing less than before, and he was now clearly following a process by which Mrs. Newsome's letters could but logically stop. . . . It struck him really that he had never so lived with her as during this period of her silence. . . . He walked about with her, sat with her, drove with her and dined face-to-face with her. . . . Her vividness . . . became . . . almost an obsession. (22:46–47)

In being invisibly yet obsessively present in Strether's mind, Mrs. Newsome attains the status of a brooding psychological force.

Later in the book, Mrs. Newsome is present somewhat more materially in the person of her daughter Sarah Pocock, who heads the second ambassadorial delegation. This delegation has been appointed to bring back not only Chad, but Strether himself. The silence that exists between Strether and the maternal Mrs. Newsome is indirectly broken when Strether has to take from Sarah a series of furious and self-righteous inquiries that escalate from " 'What is your conduct but an outrage to women like *us* [Mrs. Newsome and her]?' " (22:199), to " 'Do you consider her [Madame de Vionnet] even an apology for a decent woman?' " (22:202). Strether speaks up unshrinkingly for Madame de Vionnet and is revealed at one point to be "just checking a low vague sound, a sound which was perhaps the nearest approach his vocal chords had ever known to a growl" (22:200), though, needless to say, he does manage to "check" it. Still it does not escape Strether that if Sarah is, in some sense, her mother, he nevertheless is not actually having the scene with Mrs. Newsome: Mrs. Newsome "was reaching him somehow by the lengthened arm of the spirit, and he was having to that extent to take her into account; but he wasn't reaching her in turn, not making her take *him*; he was only reaching Sarah" (22:198). Strether's assertiveness with Sarah is finally only substitutive and, as a result, he never really calls into question or rejects his filial bond with Mrs. Newsome.

Strether's filial obedience produces in him a sense of penance as for transgression. Anticipating Sarah's arrival in Paris, he contemplates a return to Woollett in guilt-ridden imagery of juvenile correction: "He already . . . burned, under her [Sarah's] reprobation, with the blush of guilt, already consented, by way of penance, to the instant forfeiture of everything. He saw himself, under her direction, recommitted to Woollett as juvenile offenders are committed to reformatories" (22:61). What is shocking here is not only that Strether feels in need of punishment, but that he thinks of himself as a "juvenile offender" rather than an adult criminal. That is, he feels like a child who has disobeyed rather than a diplomat who, having had a change of heart, has hazarded an independent, maturely responsible reinterpretation of his mission. In the scenario, James calls Strether's return "his domestic penalty" (*Notebooks*, p. 414), a punishment as for some house chore not performed by a youngster. On his last visit to Madame de Vionnet's wondrously evocative lodgings, Strether reflects on her possessions that "he should certainly see nothing in the least degree like them. He should soon be going to where such things were not" (22:275), as though he were going into exile or to prison. Isabel Archer comes to mind when Strether speculates at the end of *The Ambassadors* that the "reckoning" ahead in Woollett may "be one and the same thing with extinction" (22:293)—the ultimate punishment.

Poirier defends Strether's renunciation of self, Paris, and the opportunities and commitments of love and sexuality by proposing that Strether has undergone a " 'conversion' . . . into a man whose capacities for appreciation create a world—alternative both to Paris and to Woollett and more compelling in the duties it demands from him than either place could be."[25] Yet this proposition would seem to require, for the sake of justice, that Strether live in neither place—or, at the least, it would not explain why it is more fitting for him to live in Woollett. It is worth noting that when James himself was faced in 1876 with the need to make a similar decision about whether to continue to reside in Paris—where he had lived since first moving to Europe, but found not entirely to his satisfaction—or to return to New England, he chose to do neither. Instead, he experimentally took up residence in London.

The end of *The Ambassadors* presents Strether's departure from Europe as a supreme instance of his filial obedience to the maternal Mrs. Newsome's imagination of his career.[26]

"All the same I must go. . . . To be right. . . . That, you see, is my only logic. Not, out of the whole affair, to have got anything for myself."

[Maria Gostrey] thought. "But with your wonderful impressions you'll have got a great deal."

"A great deal"—he agreed. "But nothing like *you*. It's you who would make me wrong!"

Honest and fine, she couldn't greatly pretend she didn't see it. Still she could pretend just a little. "But why should you be so dreadfully right?" . . .

So then she had to take it, though still with her defeated protest. "It isn't so much your *being* 'right'—it's your horrible sharp eye for what makes you so."

"Oh but you're just as bad yourself. You can't resist me when I point that out."

She sighed it at last all comically, all tragically, away. "I can't indeed resist you."

"Then there we are!" said Strether. (22:326–27)

In this last exchange, Strether shows that he has learned the art of conversation as a technique—the conversation is as artful as any in the book—but the spirit of such reciprocal talk still eludes him. Strether contrives to imply that his exchange with Maria Gostrey is open and, at the same time, to conclude it. His artfully indefinite " 'there we are' " seems to establish them in the uncharted realm of meaning-as-process, for we are certainly tempted to ask Where? Where are we? But at the same time, in an extension of his " 'only logic' " and his " 'right[ness],' " Strether is insisting that this point— " 'there' "—is the only end the conversation could come to. He had the point in mind before they began to speak. It is not simply that, having fallen in love with Madame de Vionnet, he is trying to be diplomatic with Maria Gostrey. His certitude here is closely related to the didacticism of the "Live all you can" speech. In his need to be right and his certainty that he

can definitively know what is right, no less a certainty in his
mind for Maria's qualifications " 'dreadfully right' " and
" 'horrible sharp eye for what makes you so,' " he echoes the
efforts at moral simplification of Isabel Archer and Fleda
Vetch. Now no longer in debt to Maria, Strether speaks with
her as an equal, yet he uses his talk to impose on her his point
of view: "she had to take it." The turning point, which reveals
that for all that Strether has learned, he is still only Strether,
is his assertion " 'It's you who would make me wrong.' " Maria
struggles with this assertion, but even in "pretend[ing] she
didn't see it," she accepts his terms; instead of asking him why
she would make him wrong, she asks him " 'why should you
be so dreadfully right?' " She has accepted his interpretation
of right and wrong, and can at most question him about his
allegiance to these terms, but not about their appropriateness.
Her acceptance moves her onto ground where he can definitively " 'defeat' " her at the art she has helped to teach him.

Although it would seem that in refusing to carry out Mrs.
Newsome's mission Strether would himself become the author
of his experience, his insistence on not getting anything for
himself, not profiting personally, implies that he is still pro-
totypically ambassadorial.[27] He defines his identity negatively:
merely offering resistance to her ambassadorial mission, he
proceeds in insubordinate complicity with it. He has, indeed,
been "booked, by her vision" (22:224).

Aside from Maria Gostrey, who asks Strether " 'To what
do you go home?' "(22:325) but seems ultimately to accept
his assertion that he is " 'right' " to go, only Madame de Vionnet seriously questions Strether's departure, thus performing
a valuable service for the reader. She knows that she has
wrought an incalculably great change in Strether's life, and
regards it ruefully, but she is capable, just the same, of wondering why it is not greater. Critics often suggest that Strether
leaves Europe because Madame de Vionnet and Chad have
failed to live up to his imagination of them. However, when

Madame de Vionnet says, " 'Of course you wouldn't, even if possible, and no matter what may happen to you, be near us' " (22:288), she is gently confronting Strether with the possibility that he may be failing to live up to the difference that his experience of Europe has made for him. She is able to do no more than symbolize the possibility that he may be failing to live up to *her* imagination of *him*—she cannot say this—because she collapses before him in self-apology, thus becoming the "bad woman" he had imagined her to be. In the same way, when Chad and Madame de Vionnet disguise their intimacy by going back to town with Strether instead of remaining behind alone in the Impressionistically rendered Parisian countryside, they surrender to his picture of their virtuous attachment rather than insisting on their own.

Chad goes a long way toward justifying Strether's early simplifications about Paris, even though he poses a challenge to easy judgments. Chad's desire for a career in America is perhaps understandable, but the language in which he vows to Strether not ever to leave Madame de Vionnet—" 'I give you my word of honour . . . that I'm not a bit tired of her' " (22:312)—shrinks the relationship to the liaison, distasteful and inconsequential, that Strether initially thought it to be. I do not mean that Chad is necessarily callow for anticipating that he might want, at some point, to make an ending with the French woman. After all, there is some indication that Madame de Vionnet is a maternal figure for Chad in the same way Mrs. Newsome is for Strether, an interpretation strengthened by the fact that Madame de Vionnet *is* a mother, and has a daughter of marriageable age suitable, as Strether himself notes, for Chad. It would thus, perhaps, be as important emotionally and professionally for Chad to free himself from Madame de Vionnet as I have argued it is for Strether to free himself from Mrs. Newsome, although Madame de Vionnet, who is presented as a virtually inexhaustible source, manifestly has more to offer. Even if it is right that their relationship be dissolved, however, the language Chad uses in talking to Strether about ending it seems unequal to the profundity of their intimacy as James has shown it, though Madame de Vionnet's speech seems never to betray its quality. Chad later invokes the more elegant, less crass criterion, " 'the point where the death comes in' " (22:317) to the relation as the method for recognizing when it might be time for him to leave. But that fails to alter what is at last even Strether's sense of him, that he remains, for all his change, and, after all, like Strether himself, "none the less only Chad" (22:284).

Madame de Vionnet, however, insofar as she is made to uphold Strether's original sense of morality, enacts a capitulation that sits on her like an inauthenticity. Even the fact that her affair with Chad is adulterous, which puts her under the burden of an additional possible reproach, cannot alter the sense of her quality. She has made Strether, and the reader, believe in her with the strength of her belief in herself, her personal style, and suddenly her confidence collapses. After the scene on the river, Strether hears from Maria Gostrey that Madame de Vionnet is lamenting " 'that she might have been better for you' " (22:302), as though agreeing with his disappointment. Indeed, in their final interview, the French woman strikes for Strether the improbable note of scraping self-apology:

> "What I hate is myself—when I think that one has to take so much, to be happy, out of the lives of others, and that one isn't happy even then. . . . The wretched self is always there, always making one somehow a fresh anxiety. What it comes to is that it's not, that it's never, a happiness, any happiness at all, to *take*. The only safe thing is to give." (22:282–83)

> "I happen to care what you think of me. And what you *might*," she added. "What you perhaps even did. . . . I who should have liked to seem to you—well, sublime!" (22:287–88)

Madame de Vionnet has changed Strether's life partly through her sheer demonstrated existence, and partly through the pressure of her need for him, the demands of her self. The mark against her is precisely that she is not, finally, purely self-transcendent, not an eyeball only—that she has a self for which she makes claims. In collapsing before him, she shows that she has become Stretherized, sold on his ideas of renunciation, converted to his wish " 'not, out of the whole affair, to have got anything for myself.' " She has been absorbed into the currency of his imagination—a very different matter from being included in his imagination for all that she is. In becoming the "bad woman" trying to reform, she is shrunk to a role not substantially larger than the "bad woman" herself.

James's remarks in the preface appear to link him with Strether in wariness and seeming condescension toward sexuality, "the imputably 'tempted' state":

> There was the dreadful old tradition, one of the platitudes of the human comedy, that people's moral scheme *does* break down in Paris . . . that hundreds of thousands of more or less hypocritical or more or less cynical persons annually visit the place for the sake of the probable catastrophe. . . . The revolution performed by Strether . . . was to have nothing to do with any *bêtise* of the imputably "tempted" state; he was to be thrown forward, rather . . . upon his lifelong trick of intense reflexion. (*Prefaces*, p. 316)

The only way, James implies, to save Strether from "platitude" or temptation is to wrap him in the mantle of "intense reflexion." James's response to sexuality in this passage seems to partake of the Woollett assumption that sexual experience is something predictable, something known, whether lurid or trivial, a fixed quantity easily apprehended and dismissed. He succumbs here, as Strether does in the novel, to a fixed imagination of sexuality. If Madame de Vionnet appears to collapse at the end of the book and become a "bad woman" lamenting her sins, and the gestures seem inauthentic to her character, we may say it is because she is doomed by those aspects of James and Strether's imagination that work together to project melodrama.

That James does nevertheless entertain and invite a larger response is apparent in his overall presentation of Madame de Vionnet. It is disturbing when she is made to suffer the indignity of self-apology and collapse especially because James has shown her forging with Strether the most impressive and moving illustration in the book of a spacious relationship. Yeazell's remarks about the verbal reciprocity of Maria Gostrey and Strether are more applicable to the conversation of Strether and Madame de Vionnet: "This pair often talk in sentence fragments—extending and completing one another's thoughts. . . . [They] continually echo and qualify each other's words, as the language which one chooses evokes in turn new insights in the other."[28] Together they make talk into a collaborative art. It is with Madame de Vionnet that Strether most consistently experiences what one might call double epiphanies, moments of mutual revelation that are the essence of love.

Double epiphanies are a logical culmination of James's interest in finding a way to keep self-transcendence from becoming self-absence. In a traditional epiphany, Strether might gain a sense of clarification or even revelation from losing himself in something (or someone) greater than himself. Critics who use the term "epiphany" or "privileged moment" to designate the nature of experience for Jamesian consciousness refer to the way the central characters are flooded by recognitions about the meaning of their world and their relation to it. By and large, these recognitions are seen as one-sided experiences in which, as in Emerson, the energy of the self transcends its center.[29] Some sense of a double experience, however, enters into the discussion of Philip Sicker, who speaks of moments of clairvoyant or telepathic awareness when lovers in James's later works seem to share a single consciousness. But Sicker ultimately argues that these moments dramatize a "self-obliterating fusion,"[30] rather than trigger a process of mutual self-discovery.

With Madame de Vionnet, however, Strether does not merely transcend himself; rather, Strether's energies are more his own because the French woman has received them. He is more himself by knowing another, knowing her. Their exchanges are remarkable for the awareness of each other that they not only register, but return to each other, and the enlarged recognition of self that each can thus assist the other to achieve. James restores the sense of self and other missing in the Emersonian epiphany by anchoring both in a dialectical social awareness.

Madame de Vionnet offers what is missing in Emerson, a genius for relations: "Deep and beautiful . . . her smile came back, and with the effect of making . . . [Strether] hear what he had said just as she had heard it. . . . she was . . . one of the rare women . . . whose very presence, look, voice, the mere contemporaneous *fact* of whom, from the moment it was at all presented, made a relation of mere recognition" (21:251–52). The relation that Madame de Vionnet makes irresistible for Strether is a collaboration in which it is both difficult to distinguish the self from other and impossible to forget that both are there:

"What can I do," he finally asked, "but listen to you as I promised Chadwick?"

"Ah but what I'm asking you," she quietly said, "isn't what Mr. Newsome had in mind. . . . This is my own idea and a different thing."

It gave poor Strether in truth—uneasy as it made him too—something of the thrill of a bold perception justified. "Well," he answered kindly enough, "I was sure a moment since that some idea of your own had come to you."

She seemed still to look up at him, but now more serenely. "I made out you were sure—and that helped it to come."

(21:248)

In these passages, collaboration takes the form of a double epiphany. Strether and Marie de Vionnet both recognize each other as other and affirm each other's sense of self. Madame de Vionnet "mak[es Strether] hear what he had said just as she had heard it," thus returning to him his own energies, in a form that is enhanced by her listening. And in his hearing, she finds herself: " 'I made out you were sure [that an idea of her own had come to her]—and that helped it to come.' " The miracle of hearing someone hearing you, or of sensing someone sensing you creates an echo chamber in which the experience is doubled, and ultimately multiplied without end. The presentation of a reciprocal or collaborative relation between a man and a woman, a relation devoid on each side, even if only verbally, of both tyrannical self-absorption and empathic self-effacement, is one of the most memorable accomplishments of *The Ambassadors*, and one of the most revolutionary in all of James. Such communication is the principal adventure of Paris for Strether and represents civilization at its peak. It joins American naturalness to European cultivation in making the case that the natural self may be not only immeasurably enriched, but actually made more capable of naturalness, through the civilized world of art and artifice.

The belief in the potential benevolence of art is paramount in James among the major nineteenth-century American novelists. Cooper, Hawthorne, Melville (most explicitly in *The Confidence Man*), and Twain regarded art and civilization as a source of dishonesty, if not corruption, as they also regarded the European influence with which art and civilization were associated. Of the earlier writers, Twain perhaps came closest to reconciling his suspicion of art with his identity as an artist when he set Huck on the raft naked in chapter 19 of *Huckleberry Finn*, and put into his mouth the celebrated paean to the river whose fidelity to nature sets it apart from the doctored treatment of nature found in art up to that time. Twain aimed at creating an unartful, unfallen art, but he could not keep Huck or his language in that state of naked originality, and Huck quickly lapses back into the civilized and compromising language of the shore society. Ultimately, no one of these writers as closely challenged his distrust of art as James did when he created Marie de Vionnet or, later, Maggie Verver. In embracing artfulness, James helped heal the split between American and European literature which had developed among American writers especially since Emerson, and thus established a precedent for the new literary fusions which eventually led, through Pound and Eliot, to modernism.

Even in their last scene together, when she strikes him as "older . . . to-night, visibly less exempt from the touch of time," Madame de Vionnet is, as always for Strether, "the finest and subtlest creature, the happiest apparition, it had been given him, in all his years, to meet" (22:286). She ages, but unlike Maria Gostrey, never declines to the maternal for him. She remains the primary and unarguable romantic relation of his life. They conclude on a note ambiguously rich but, for Strether, inhibiting in its allusions to sexuality, and its associations of sexuality with fraud. Strether makes the pun that introduces the element of fraud: " 'What's cheerful for *me*,' she replied, 'is that we might, you and I, have been friends. That's it—that's it. You see how, as I say, I want everything. I've wanted you too.' 'Ah but you've *had* me!' he declared, at the door, with an emphasis that made an end" (22:288–89). To Maria, Strether confesses that Marie de Vionnet's idea that she and he might have been friends is "just . . . why I'm going" (22:303). Madame de Vionnet represents a vision of sexuality for which Strether and James are unprepared, and James here gives in to distrust of her seductive artfulness, a distrust which much of his late work modulates in the reconciliation of artfulness and truth. In this case, however, James limits the threat of Marie de Vionnet's appeal by having Strether convert her into the currency of his devaluing pun, and leave her.

Strether is unable to embody his verbal collaboration with Madame de Vionnet in any permanent or material form, to make a reciprocally *lived* fiction out of it, because he is bound to his " 'only logic' " (22:326), renunciation. The result of this logic is a continuing commitment to acts of substitution. Not only does he instruct Chad to reject Woollett instead of rejecting it himself—an effort to sustain his own filial rebellion through Chad—but he charges Chad to remain faithful to Madame de Vionnet, using language that is unaccountably strong for a detached spectator: " 'You'll be a brute, you know—you'll be guilty of the last infamy—if you ever forsake her' " (22:308). He exhorts Chad, in effect, as though for some cause of his own: " 'Let me . . . appeal to you by all you hold sacred. . . . You'd not only be, as I say, a brute; you'd be . . . a criminal of the deepest dye' " (22:311). Strether's urgency betrays a didactic impulse not far removed from the moral purpose with which he first went to Paris. Between instructing Chad that he must leave Madame de Vionnet, and instructing him that he must not, between viewing Marie de Vionnet as the villainess and viewing Chad as the villain (a " 'brute,' " a " 'criminal' "), there is principally the difference that in the first case, Strether is acting for Mrs. Newsome and, in the second, he is trying to make Chad act for him.

Strether's substitutive concern with Chad's behavior is similar to Isabel's concern for Pansy. In both cases, the interests of the self can only be expressed decenteredly, through an interest in what is outside of the self. The strenuousness of Strether's language to Chad reveals an effort to impose a fiction on the book that will enact his own attachment to Madame de Vionnet without his having to experience it himself. But his absence from the design that he wishes to promote, which follows inevitably from his absence from his own desires, means that he cannot be accountable for what finally will happen to Madame de Vionnet. Only Strether's own presence could secure Marie de Vionnet from abandonment.

IN THE CAGE

James's 1898 novella *In the Cage* presents another view of ambassadorship and collaborative relations. Although it precedes *The Ambassadors* compositionally, *In the Cage* issues in an alternative to self-transcendence that looks forward to *The Golden Bowl*. Considering its quality and the importance conferred on it by James's decision to include it in the New York edition of his work, criticism of the piece is surprisingly scarce. Moreover, the criticism that has been written largely ignores the revolutionary dimension constituted by the plot's interrogation of its own ambassadorial theme.

The heroine of the story appears initially to inhabit several different cages. She is the prisoner not only of poverty and low class, and of the barred "cage" in which she works as a telegraphist, but also of consciousness and of the sexual melodrama in which consciousness traps her. In the telegraph cage, her imagination takes flight for a time, her consciousness of others stimulated by her social and occupational isolation. In the novella's preface, James looks back on Hyacinth Robinson in *The Princess Casamassima*, who is released, as it seems, from the cage of confining social realities, like poverty and low class, in the first part of that book, into consciousness in the second. In *In the Cage*, however, James shows that consciousness itself may be a cage from which character needs to be rescued. The action of the story is devoted to exploring how far out of that cage the telegraphist can escape, both as a woman and a figure of imagination.

As a telegraphist, the heroine is an ambassador, delegated to transmit messages from one party to another, employed on behalf of others rather than self-employed. Her response to customers is to imagine, on the basis of their coded messages, plots for their lives which then occupy a central position in her own consciousness. Thus, Lady Bradeen

> had come in for Everard [the two are secretly lovers]. . . . If our young lady had never taken such jumps before it was simply that she had never before been so affected. . . . Mary and Cissy [aliases for Lady Bradeen] had been round together, in their single superb person, to see him—he must live round the corner; they had found that, in consequence of something they had come, precisely, to make up for or to have another scene about, he had gone off . . . on which they had come together to Cocker's [the grocery store, half of which is a telegraph office] . . . where they had put in the three forms partly in order not to put in the one alone. . . . Oh yes, she went all the way, and this was a specimen of how she often went.
> (11:378–79)

James portrays the telegraphist as an avid reader of "ha'penny a day" novels, lurid romances "all about fine folks" (11:367), which provide the models for her own authorial propensities. When she meets Captain Everard outside of the cage, she describes the appeal of staying on at Cocker's in melodramatic literary terms borrowed from these novels of passion: " 'I recognise at Cocker's certain strong attractions. All you people come. I like all the horrors. . . . Your extravagance, your selfishness, your immorality, your crimes. . . . I revel in them' "
(11:446–47).

Tony Tanner sees *In the Cage* as a story of the Jamesian artist as observer,[31] and at first, the growth of the heroine's imagination does seem to be the result of an absence from experience. It is clear that she has feelings for Everard which would be appropriate to a relationship of her own with him, but she declines to create such a reality, as she could if she met him outside of the cage. Instead, she fantasizes fulfillment, something which Fleda and Strether do not permit themselves to do.

> She quite thrilled herself with thinking what, with such a lot of material [as she has culled from taking telegraphic messages], a bad girl would do. It would be a scene better than many in her ha'penny novels, this going to him in the dusk of evening at Park Chambers and letting him at last have it. "I know too much about a certain person now not to put it to you—excuse my being so lurid—that it's quite worth your while to buy me off. Come therefore: buy me!" There was a point indeed at which such flights had to drop again—the point of an unreadiness to name, when it came to that, the purchasing medium. It wouldn't certainly be anything so gross as money, and the matter accordingly remained rather vague, all the more that *she* was not a bad girl. (11:417)

Yet although the fantasy allows sexual desire to enter the realm of consciousness, consciousness itself becomes imprisoning when it prevents her from having the reality of passion. When she meets Everard one evening outside of the telegraph cage, the fear of playing the melodramatic role of bad girl projected in her consciousness inhibits her impulse to invent a more personal relationship with him almost as well as have the bars of Cocker's cage:

> "I'd do anything for you. I'd do anything for you." Never in her life had she known anything so high and fine as this, just letting him have it and bravely and magnificently leaving it. Didn't the place, the associations and circumstances [a park bench at night where they are surrounded by amorous couples on other benches], perfectly make it sound what it wasn't? and wasn't that exactly the beauty? (11:442)

It might almost seem that the heroine is genuinely reinventing the possibilities of such scenes were it not for the tortured logic of her speech, its exaggerated rhapsodic language, and the scared "primness" of her theatrical departure: "When she watched herself, in the memory of that night, walk away from him as if she were making an end, she found something too pitiful in the primness of such a gait" (11:462).

In the cage of consciousness, the girl's desires have been held in an equilibrium in which she could both brush up against sexuality and be safe from it. Meeting at Cocker's has been " 'as if there were something—I don't know what to call it!—between us. I mean something unusual and good and awfully nice—something not a bit horrid or vulgar' " (11: 441). She has had a relationship with the captain, even in some ways an intimate one (through his telegrams, she has entered his private life), but on the safely isolated terms set by consciousness. As in *The Portrait*, James seems to be interested in the detrimental implications of traditional metaphors for sexuality: here, the box. The term *box* originally referred only to a theater compartment but its use was extended around 1700 to include the occupants of the boxes, in particular the ladies. James describes his heroine at work in the cage as "so boxed up with her young men" (11:396), a use of the metaphor that encourages reconsideration of the aptness of an image for female sexuality which evokes so strong a sense of claustrophobia and limitation. The language perfectly questions the telegraphist's cloistered eroticism in Cocker's cage and the cage of her imagination.

With the news that Everard is about to marry Lady Bradeen, who has suddenly been widowed, this heroine, like others in James, experiences her suffering and deprivation in the cherishing syntax of parallel clauses: "his having sat with her there on the bench and under the trees in the summer darkness and put his hand on her, making her know what he would have said if permitted; his having returned to her afterwards, repeatedly [at Cocker's], with supplicating eyes and fever in his blood; and her having on her side, hard and pedantic . . . only answered him, yet supplicating back, through the bars of the cage" (11:503).

Although its restraints will be mitigated by her fiancé's ambitiousness, the cage of poverty and class will remain: "Reality, for the poor things they both were [she and her friend Mrs. Jordan], could only be ugliness and obscurity, could never be the escape, the rise" (11:499). At the end of the story the young woman disappears from view in a dense fog, making blindly, in the style of Isabel, "a few sightless turns" (11:507). L. C. Knights mourns the heroine's return to "the bleakness of reality" with her still "caged . . . excluded consciousness." Morton Dauwen Zabel puts the heroine in the company of James's "caged, or pinioned" characters who snatch from loss or exclusion "the trophy of the spirit's 'vitality.' "[32] When critics invite us to see in the end of the work a picture of the heroine standing lonely guard over consciousness, or stress her return to the bleak social reality of her class, they are asking us to see her as a victim in a melodrama. Yet to do so is hardly to catch sight of the ultimately robust young woman altering the boundaries of her enclosures.

For in *In the Cage*, two stories intersect. The first is the typical James plot about the renouncing heroine who discounts herself and loses the possibility of romance and agency in the social world. The second plot, looking forward to *What Maisie Knew* and *The Golden Bowl*, concerns a heroine who is rescued from the melodramatic fiction in which her consciousness imprisons her, in this case by accepting an alternate suitor, the grocer Mr. Mudge. James shows that the Everard the telegraphist finds glamorous is actually a cad, a revelation which, as in *The Sacred Fount*, implies that when the empathic imagination is totally predicated on *self*-transcendence, it is incomplete and unreliable about *other*. As Jean Frantz Blackall notes, "One of James's ironies is simply that the great world the girl

112

envisions is not necessarily the one she would find."[33] The information that emerges in support of the captain's crudity and the telegraphist's narrative unreliability has the effect of propelling us beyond the first plot and preparing us to care more about the second.

James thus makes audible an insensitive banality in the jolly unspoken speech that the heroine attributes to Everard without reproof: " 'Don't put yourself out any longer,' he would say, 'for so bad a case. . . . I thank and acquit and release you. Our lives take us. I don't know much—though I've really been interested—about yours, but I suppose you've got one. Mine at any rate will take *me*—and where it will. Heigh-ho! Good-bye.' " (11:474). During his last visit to the cage, he speaks to the heroine apparently without the slightest conscious memory of who she is, or of their park communion: "He really spoke to her as if she had been some strange young woman at Knightsbridge or Paddington [other branches of the post office]" (11:477). When her memory of a crucial telegram enables her to rescue him from a crisis, he leaves "without another look, without a word of thanks, without time for anything or anybody" (11:484). Later she discovers, to her amazement, that the captain has scandalously compromised Lady Bradeen, and that he not only is not rich, but because of debts "he has nothing" (11:502). And thus, whereas Fleda's loss of Owen, who is sometimes gauche but nevertheless sensitive, is movingly presented as an occasion for grief, even though that grief might have been avoided, the telegraphist's loss of Everard is made to seem a stroke of luck.

The telegraphist's preference for encagement at first makes it seem likely that her approaching marriage to the banally named Mr. Mudge will be an extension of life in the cage, rather than an escape from it. If we get over our surprise that she marries at all, given the isolation of most James protagonists, we expect, at the least, to witness the spectacle of a marriage like Isabel and Osmond's that is itself isolating and imprisoning. But the novella proves resistant to the melo-dramatically reduced ha'penny analyses of conduct in which the heroine indulges. She marries someone whose singular capacity for surprising her helps them reinvent together the emotional space between them. In the process, the heroine escapes from the cage of her imagination in which she has kept herself genteelly separate from experience. The novella thus may easily be seen as a story quintessentially about wom-en's experience. In it, James contemplates the possibility of women successfully escaping from imprisoning feminine stereotypes.

That Mudge has numerous failings is obvious even from the stodginess of this name. Criticism of the tale tends either to neglect him altogether or to dismiss him with passing ref-erence. Zabel speaks disparagingly of "the dull marriage with Mr. Mudge,"[34] and Charles Thomas Samuels mistakenly grants him only the "appeal . . . accurately suggested by his name."[35] The heroine thinks about her fiancé in pinched and homely metaphors of scraped plates and "contracted" space.

> He had at any rate ceased to be all day long in her eyes [he has left Cocker's for employment at Chalk Farm], and this left something a little fresh for them to rest on of a Sunday. . . . she had often asked herself what . . . marriage would be able to add to a familiarity that seemed already to have scraped the platter so clean. Opposite there [in the grocery with which the telegraph office shares the premises of Cocker's] . . . he had moved to and fro before her as on the small sanded floor of their contracted future. She was conscious now of the im-provement of not having to take her present and her future at once. (11:368–69)

She thinks of her fiancé's epistolary communications from Chalk Farm as "the daily deadly flourishy letter from Mr. Mudge" (11:373), and acknowledges to herself that "His very

beauty was the beauty of a grocer. . . . She had engaged herself
in short to the perfection of a type" (11:405).

When Mudge first asks her why she is not ready to leave
Cocker's for a life with him at Chalk Farm, she explains her
reluctance in terms of the appeal to her imagination: " 'Where
I am I still see things.' " She revises her assessment that "he
hadn't enough imagination to oblige her" when she sees that
he is surprisingly receptive: "Little by little, to her own stu-
pefaction, she caught that he was trying to take it [her ex-
planation] as she meant it and that he was neither astonished
nor angry" (11:406). This is impressive, even though her stu-
pefaction receives a check at the discovery that his receptivity
may be an aspect of his type: "What she had done was simply
to give his sensibility another push into the dim vast of trade.
In that direction it was all alert and she had whisked before
it the mild fragrance of a 'connexion.' That was the most he
could see in any account of her keeping in, on whatever
roundabout lines, with the gentry" (11:406–7). Through comic
use of epigram, James gives an indication of Mudge's voice
that again reveals his "perfection of . . . type": "What really
touched him . . . was that she could . . . keep before him . . .
the very wind of the swift bank-notes and the charm of the
existence of a class that Providence had raised up to be the
blessing of grocers. . . . the exuberance of the aristocracy was
the advantage of trade. . . . The more flirtations, as he might
roughly express it, the more cheese and pickles" (11:409–10).

Even Mudge's moral sense conforms to the limitations of
grocery epigram: "Above all it hurt him somewhere—for he
had his private delicacies—to see anything *but* money made
out of his betters. To be too enquiring, or in any other way
too free, at the expense of the gentry was vaguely wrong; the
only thing that was distinctly right was to be prosperous at
any price" (11:410–11). Breaking down the substance of his
fiancée's consciousness into digestibly familiar material,
Mudge shows that he is the hostage of his commercial met-

aphors as much as she is the prisoner of her metaphors of sexual melodrama.

Initially the source of Mudge's impressiveness for the heroine is his ability to leave the cage, whether to settle an argument or to change employment. She recalls a decisive scene in which the grocer was able to "step round the counter," an act of comparative daring which the heroine and others who work at Cocker's find beyond them:

> She had once . . . seen him collar a drunken soldier, a big violent man who, having come in with a mate to get a postal-order cashed, had made a grab at the money before his friend could reach it and had so determined . . . immediate and alarming reprisals. . . . Mr. Buckton and the counter-clerk had crouched within the cage, and Mr. Mudge had, with a very quiet but very quick step round the counter, an air of masterful authority she shouldn't soon forget, triumphantly interposed in the scrimmage, parted the combatants and shaken the delinquent in his skin. . . . if their affair [the engagement] had not already been settled the neatness of his execution would have left her without resistance. (11:404)

At the end of a joint holiday at Bournemouth, when Mudge reveals that he has been handsomely promoted at Chalk Farm and has even spotted a suitable home for them, the heroine reflects with some awe that "His having kept this great news for the last . . . and not floated it out in the current of his chatter and the luxury of their leisure, was one of those incalculable strokes by which he could still affect her; the kind of thing that reminded her of the latent force that had ejected the drunken soldier. . . . Mr. Mudge was distinctly her fate" (11:455). The tone invites us to patronize the couple a little, but if such a fate is small, it is still admirably full of "incalculable strokes." What it means for Mudge to be the girl's fate is that it is her fate to be surprised, not, as with Isabel, to suffer.

Not least of the several ways in which Mudge is associated with an escape from confinement is his rescue of the telegraphist from the cage in which her stereotypes about female sexuality imprison her. At Bournemouth, she finally spells out for her fiancé the appeal of staying on at Cocker's:

> "I went out the other night and sat in the Park with a gentleman," she said at last.
>
> Nothing was ever seen like his confidence in her; and she wondered a little now why it didn't irritate her. It only gave her ease and space, as she felt, for telling him the whole truth that no one knew. . . . "And what did you get from that?" he asked with a concern that was not in the least for his honour.
>
> (11:456)

By giving her a sense of "space," he helps her out of her confining consciousness. At the same time, Mudge himself is given a sense of space by her challenge to the habitually commercial confines of his imagination. Although he wants to know what she gets, acquisitively speaking, from the experience she narrates, he consents, as they continue talking, to enter her world of immaterial satisfactions:

> "You ought perhaps to know . . . exactly what I told him. That I'd do anything for him."
>
> "What do you mean by 'anything'?"
>
> "Everything."
>
> Mr. Mudge's immediate comment on this statement was to draw from his pocket a crumpled paper containing the remains of half a pound of "sundries". . . . "Have another?—*that* one," he said. She had another, but not the one he indicated, and then he continued: "What took place afterwards? . . . "
>
> "I simply came away . . . leaving him there. I didn't let him follow me."
>
> "Then what did you let him do?"
>
> "I didn't let him do anything."

Mr. Mudge considered an instant. "Then what did you go there for?" His tone was even slightly critical.

"I didn't quite know at the time. It was simply to be with him, I suppose—just once. . . . It makes meeting him—at Cocker's, since it's that I want to stay on for—more interesting."

"It makes it mighty interesting for *me!*" Mr. Mudge freely declared. "Yet he didn't follow you?" he asked. "*I* would!"

(11:457–58)

Mudge's assertion of sexual aggressiveness—" '*I* would!' "—makes natural and permissible the telegraphist's tacit sexuality. Prompted by elements in her narrative which he openly regards as erotic, he collaborates with her to produce a second version of the meeting with Everard. His train of questions acceptingly projects, beyond the confines of what she actually allowed to happen, a plot that inclines remarkably in the direction of the telegraphist's sexual fantasies, but without giving in to their melodrama about horrors and bad girls.

Everard's appeal falters while Mudge's credit grows beyond the flourishing banality for which it is easy to dismiss him. The grocer's commercial vigor will help the girl escape a life of dire poverty, and his collaborative presence helps her out of the cage of consciousness and the imagination of sexual melodrama which would otherwise create for her a life of solitude and suffering. At Bournemouth, the telegraphist had at first found that spending time with Mudge was precisely a matter of solitude, a matter of "secret conversations. This separate commerce was with herself" (11:453). The pun on "commerce" associates material with immaterial gain, profitable joint transactions with isolated self-communion, oppositions which the novella suggests the telegraphist can perhaps ultimately bridge as a result of a union with Mudge.

In rejecting the cage, as invoked by James with the phrase "separate commerce," the girl seeks a way out of the stereotypically feminine polarity that keeps consciousness separate from the world. James self-consciously talks about this split when he distinguishes, in the preface to *Daisy Miller*, between an uptown world of sensitive, internalized experience presided over by women and children, and a downtown world of money and outwardly aggressive, external forms of experience presided over my men (*Prefaces*, pp. 272–75): in effect, the two kinds of commerce implied in the pun. James's conception of the opposition in terms that are close to those of contemporary feminism and feminist thinking on androgyny is suggested in his 1902 essay "Matilde Serao." There, in discussing the differences between men and women writers, James speaks of "man's relations with himself, that is with woman":

> The female mind has in fact throughout the competition [writing fiction] carried off the prize in the familiar game, known to us all from childhood's hour, of playing at "grown-up;" finding thus its opportunity . . . in the more and more marked tendency of the mind of the other gender to revert . . . to those simplicities which there would appear to be some warrant for pronouncing puerile [the reference is to the tendency of male writers to take as their subject man's "relations with the pistol, the pirate, the police, the wild and the tame beast"]. It is the ladies in a word who have lately done most to remind us of man's relations with himself, that is with woman.[36]

In this startlingly modern formulation, male and female are at once separate sexes and two potentially harmonious parts of a single collaborative whole. The estrangement of consciousness from the material world, which is associated with the failure of "man's relations with himself" and the failure of "man's relations . . . with woman," is thus a feminist concern in James whether it occurs in a female character or a "poor sensitive gentleman" (*Prefaces*, p. 246). If James invites us to take a strongly farcical interest in Mudge and the telegraphist, he also shows them attempting a variety of collaborations whose importance, poignancy, and originality bring them out, as they bring the Assinghams in *The Golden Bowl*, somewhere beyond farce.

—4—

"Imagination in *Predominance*"

Like Fleda Vetch, Strether, and the young telegraphist, six-year-old Maisie Farange is trapped in ambassadorial service. *What Maisie Knew* (1897) begins when a divorce court assigns the child to alternating terms with parents who use her as "a messenger of insult." Once she has "puzzled out . . . that everything was bad because she had been employed to make it so" (11:15) by her parents, she begins to repudiate their ambassadorial "employment," to have her own feelings, and to employ them for her own purposes. At the end of the novel, rejecting the alien designs for her life that confine her in the novel's various parental houses, Maisie grows up. The intricate five-way custody battle that develops over the course of the book concludes for Maisie at the edge of adolescence with what amounts to an act of self-custody, as she struggles to achieve the "imagination in *predominance*" that will enable her to possess the material of her life in a plot of her own design.

Maisie rejects her parents' ambassadorial conception of her life at first through resistance, a refusal to report what one of them has instructed her to say against the other: she begins with "the idea of an inner self or, in other words, of concealment. . . . Her parted lips locked themselves with the determination to be employed no longer" (11:15). It is clear what she does not want, but not what she does. The merely negative assertion of self involved in her silence perpetuates her helplessness:

> The sharpened sense of spectatorship was the child's main support, the long habit, from the first, of seeing herself in discussion [by other people] and finding in the fury of it—she had a glimpse of the game of football—a sort of compensation for the doom of a peculiar passivity. It gave her often an odd air of being present at her history in as separate a manner as if she could only get at experience by flattening her nose against a pane of glass. (11:107)

The effect is as though her life existed outside of and apart from her. She is the football, passively taking direction from the will of other people. But her consciousness is not even in the football—it is watching from the other side of the pane of glass.

Yet Maisie's silence, looking forward to Maggie Verver's in *The Golden Bowl,* is ultimately reinventive. Her "idea of an inner self," cultivated in silence, is in part the same idea that comes to Strether with his disobedient determination to see for himself, and to Catherine Sloper in tentative excursions into dissimulation in a few exchanges with her father and Aunt Penniman. But beyond a certain point in Catherine's verbal evasions, as in her silences, and in the silences of Claire de Cintré, Isabel, Fleda, and Strether, feelings are not found but lost. Maisie's "locked lips," however, prepare for her escape from an emotional life melodramatically manipulated in her by others, even though they seem to associate her with a kind of Jamesian consciousness that never explicitly authorizes the expression of anger.

Consciously resisting one kind of parental employment, the transmission of insult, Maisie is then for a long time the unconscious agent of another: she finds herself unintentionally promoting liaisons for her parents' benefit. First she brings together her beautiful governess Miss Overmore and her father Beale, who later marry. Then she brings together the new Mrs. Beale and Sir Claude, the compassionate and romantic figure her mother has recently married. But this unconscious gift for composition is not fully at Maisie's own disposal, for the new parental pairs prove to be as manipulative, perhaps also as derelict, as the old. They use their connection with the child to promote their own designs—to begin and conceal the affairs, or to give them an air of respectability— while Maisie, unable to exert supreme imaginative command, is trapped and neglected in the architecture of multiplying relations that she has invented.

James himself uses Maisie in the novel's preface in some of the same ways that her various parents use her in the novel. For instance, he speaks of her functioning as a tool of his novelistic design: "Instead of simply submitting to the inherited tie and the imposed complication, of suffering from them, our little wonder-working agent would create . . . quite fresh elements of this order" (*Prefaces*, p. 142). As a "little wonder-working agent" of James's "order," Maisie is converted from a character into what Bersani calls a "technical ingenuity."[1] Another passage also illustrates the way the prefaces often diminish the emotional impact of the novels. "Not less than the chance of misery and of a degraded state, the chance of happiness and of an improved state might be . . . involved for the child, round about whom the complexity of life would thus turn to fineness, to richness—and indeed would have but so to turn for the small creature to be steeped in security and ease" (*Prefaces*, p. 141). Readers fresh from the novel may have trouble recalling any impression of "the small creature," even at the end, "steeped in security and ease." Both this remade version of the plot and the one that disposes of her as a structural functionary in the novel might be said to constitute parental houses of fiction in which Maisie does not seem to fit.

James's anesthetized tone toward Maisie in the preface resembles the objectifying way society talks or sounds at the beginning of the novel. With the jargonistic and impersonal voices of the law, finance, and gossip, the book's prologue renders what will become the increasingly subjective and intimate world of Maisie's experience from an initially external perspective. It is reported in the prologue's Latinate legal voice, for example, that "the litigation [of the divorce and custody proceedings] had seemed interminable" (11:3). And when Beale is unable to refund to Ida some money that he owes her, and the court stipulates that each parent support Maisie in turn, it is said that by this "partition of the tutelary office" Beale's debt is "remitted" to him. We hear too of "people . . . looking for appeals in the newspapers for the rescue of the little one" (11:4), also called "the bone of contention" (11:5), language whose preciosity is not far removed from the prefatory coyness of "little wonder-working agent." James informs us that Maisie lives in "a society in which for the most part people were occupied only with chatter" (11:6), a species of talk which, like that in *Washington Square* and *The Awkward Age,* is disconnected from felt emotion. Just as the abstract and technical voice of the prefaces often anesthetizes the experience of the novels, the various voices of society in *Maisie* forge a variety of talk that betrays the sources of feeling James ultimately makes most important. Though *Maisie* begins, in the vein of *Washington Square,* with the brittle ironies generated by remote and superficial views of the heroine's experience, it proceeds to shield her from both irony and melodrama by anchoring itself in her deepening sense of self.[2] That is, she escapes from the rhetorically glib versions of her experience presented in the prologue and the preface by locating in herself the felt emotion absent from their styles. In doing so, she is ultimately able to outgrow all of the parental fictions in which the novel threatens to imprison her. She gets away a little even from the house of fiction that James erects for his heroine in his own voice in the preface.

Maisie's release from her parents is managed in scenes that free her from them both physically and emotionally. Ida is relieved that Sir Claude has abducted Maisie from her custody because it saves her the inconvenience of continuing to have the child in her life. But Maisie distills most of the sting from Ida's desire to abandon her when she has a scene with the captain, Ida's latest lover, in which she discovers the measure of sincerely positive feeling that she has for her mother beyond dread, or mystified awe, or pain. The captain reports about Ida: " 'She's tremendous fun—she can do all sorts of things better than I've ever seen anyone. . . . She has the nerve for a tiger-shoot. . . . Look here, she's *true!*' " (11:151). If the virtues the captain celebrates are scarcely maternal and barely accurate, that hardly matters since

> What it appeared to . . . [Maisie] to come to was that on the subject of her ladyship it was the first real kindness she had heard, so that at the touch of it something strange and deep and pitying surged up within her. . . . She cried, with a pang, straight *at* him. . . . "Oh do you love her?" . . .
> . . . "Of *course* I love her, damn it, you know!"
> . . . "So do *I* then. I do, I do, I do!" (11:151-53)

Maisie has a brief opportunity to feel authentically loving toward her father too in a scene in which Beale abandons her by trying to make her say she does not want him. The scene with Ida's captain and the one with Beale are corresponding moments at the heart of the novel in which Maisie is released from her parents in the most profound sense, even from the impression of hurt.

Maisie's scene with her father begins when he abducts her

and takes her, oedipally, to his mistress's rooms. Alone with him there,

> Maisie had her sense . . . of her having grown for him. . . . There was a passage during which, on a yellow silk sofa under one of the palms, he had her on his knee, stroking her hair, playfully holding her off while he showed his shining fangs and let her, with a vague affectionate helpless pointless "Dear old girl, dear little daughter," inhale the fragrance of his cherished beard. . . . it needed nothing more than this to make up to her in fact for omissions. The tears came into her eyes again as they had done when in the Park that day the Captain told her so "splendidly" that her mother was good. What was this but splendid too—this still direster goodness of her father . . . out of which everything had dropped but that he was papa and that he was magnificent? (11:180)

Though Beale, like Ida, does not in fact deserve Maisie's generosity, he nevertheless, however unintentionally, helps release his daughter from the hold of childhood memories of suffering, as Catherine Sloper is never fully released. Nor for all his "shining fangs" does Beale loom in Maisie's imagination with the melodramatic power that Osmond possesses for Pansy and Isabel. Maisie is no longer her parents' victim not only because she escapes them physically but, more profoundly, because she ceases to regard them as damaging.

With her actual parents out of the picture, the last third of the novel shows Maisie reassembling in Boulogne with her stepparents, Sir Claude and Mrs. Beale, and her current governess Mrs. Wix. Her governess favors a living arrangement that excludes Mrs. Beale; she wishes to save Maisie from what she regards as the corrupting effect of daily exposure to adultery. Sir Claude, however, proposes a household composed of Maisie, Mrs. Beale, and himself, minus the didactic Mrs. Wix. Pressed to choose between these alternatives, Maisie is

caught between the possibility that the stepparents care about
her for herself, and the alternate or perhaps overlapping
possibility that they care for her largely because her presence
gives their relationship an appearance of respectability.

An earlier exchange between Maisie and Beale about the
stepparents has made clear that in the *Maisie* world, the impulses of caring and the architecture of use are hard to tell
apart but difficult to combine for any length of time:

> "They're probably the worst people in the world and the
> very greatest criminals," Beale pleasantly urged. . . .
> "Well, it doesn't prevent them from loving me. They love
> me tremendously." . . .
> . . . "You're a jolly good pretext . . . for their game." . . .
> The child reflected. "Well then that's all the more reason
> . . . for their being kind to me."
> . . . "Don't you understand," Beale pursued, "that . . . they'll
> just simply chuck you? . . . they'll cease to require you." . . .
> . . . "Cease to require me because they won't care?"
>
> (11:189–90)

The novel's consideration of the authenticity of emotion beneath stylishness boils down to the question of whether Sir
Claude is a fraud. It is one of the book's brilliant strokes that
this question, like the one of how we are to regard Charlotte
and Amerigo's adultery in *The Golden Bowl,* is never conclusively resolved. Sir Claude's desires and motives are so mixed,
there are so many feelings that need to be honored, that it is
almost as difficult to convict him of actual dishonesty as it is
Madame de Vionnet.

Maisie finally grasps "the implication of a kind of natural
divergence between lovers and little girls" (11:204) in a supremely unstable society that makes people choose between
being lovers and being parents—a divergence which, paradoxically, exists even though it is she who has brought the

lovers together. She realizes that if she were to forsake Mrs. Wix and accept Sir Claude's proposal that she live with him and Mrs. Beale, the cycle of composition and abandonment in which she has been victimized might reassert itself. This realization makes her counter Sir Claude's proposal with one of her own: that they go away together, just the two of them. The importance of her locating a desiring self, and articulating this desire in the form of a design, can hardly be overemphasized. James says, "She knew what she wanted. All her learning and learning had made her at last learn that" (11:357).

At the train station, she and Sir Claude very nearly do depart by themselves:

> "I wish we could go. Won't you take me?"
> He continued to smile. "Would you really come?"
> "Oh yes, oh yes. Try." . . .
> Sir Claude turned to a porter. "When does the train go?"
> . . . "In two minutes. *Monsieur est placé? . . . Et vos billets?*" . . .
> Then after a look at Maisie, *"Monsieur veut-il que je les prenne?"* the man said.
> Sir Claude turned back to her. *"Veux-tu bien qu'il en prenne?"*
> It was the most extraordinary thing in the world: in the intensity of her excitement she not only by illumination understood all their French, but fell into it with an active perfection. She addressed herself straight to the porter. *"Prenny, prenny. Oh prenny!"* (11:344–45)

Although the train departs on her hauntingly plaintive invocation of a new version of the plot and their relationship, Maisie for the first time has found her voice: " '*Prenny, prenny. Oh prenny.*' " The French, just improvised, suggests that there has been no place in the language they customarily speak for the expression of her personally desiring self; until now, indeed, there have been no words for it at all. Yet if Maisie can thus speak her desire, she cannot, like Maggie Verver, impose it. The upshot of Maisie's success at locating a self with hopes and needs of its own and proposing to Sir Claude a design that fulfills these is that, although Sir Claude is tempted, he finds it impossible to accede. He cannot give up Mrs. Beale. To a degree that undermines her imaginative authority, Maisie's material exhibits its own "germinal property and authority."

But although Maisie is unable to enforce the version of the plot she prefers—that is, life with Sir Claude—she can nevertheless place herself beyond melodrama by escaping from his household, *his* fiction. Catherine Sloper, like Maisie, cultivates through silence a desiring self: she pursues a marriage with Morris despite her father's opposition. Once that design proves impossible to realize, however, she collapses back into her father's fiction of her. Morris was in so many ways like her father that desiring him hardly even constituted a new design. Maisie, on the other hand, makes a convincingly complete exit from the novel's oedipal drama.

For Beale, her actual father, when he holds her on his knee, strokes her hair, murmurs in her ear, and offers her the scent of "his cherished beard," Maisie is no longer a mere child. For her stepfather Sir Claude, the growing Maisie is similarly both a woman and a child, a potential sweetheart and a daughter; he shares the confusion of Beale's " 'Dear old girl, dear little daughter.' " He even repeats Beale's symbolically sexual abduction with another of his own when he sweeps Maisie off to Boulogne and nearly elopes with her on the train. In bidding for control of the meanings she inadvertently made possible when she brought Mrs. Beale and Sir Claude together, Maisie seeks to secure what she has always yearned for, a measure of emotional safety. But it does not follow that she is trying to have Sir Claude strictly as a parent when she proposes that they depart together on the train.

The extent of Maisie's sexual maturity has been a major issue in criticism of the novel. F. R. Leavis, for example, contends that Maisie's adoration of Sir Claude is safely "feminine," but not at all sexual.[3] Harris Wilson, however, has read Maisie's feelings for Sir Claude as incestuously sexual: "Her greatest asset opposed to Mrs. Beale's lush worldliness is her virginity, and that she is prepared to offer" to Sir Claude if they go away together.[4] Edward Wasiolek accepts the sexuality implicit in Maisie's proposal to Sir Claude,[5] but does not consider how the collapse of Maisie's projected scenario actually assists her toward sexual maturity. Similarly, Muriel G. Shine, tracing the movement toward maturity in James's fictional children, blames Sir Claude for sticking with Mrs. Beale,[6] and thus overlooks the potential for growth in Maisie's separation from him.

It seems very unlikely that James concerned himself with the question of whether or not Maisie might go to bed with Sir Claude. It does, however, seem likely—especially in the context of Catherine Sloper, Isabel, and Strether's damaging attachment to parental figures and their fictions—that James was concerned in *Maisie* with the obstacles to sexual and imaginative maturity posed by oedipal irresolution. The difference in this respect between *Maisie* and the earlier works is that the oedipal attachment is initially acknowledged as something natural. Commenting on Maisie's early admission to Mrs. Wix that she is in love with her stepfather, James avers that "Everything was as it should be" (11:74). This both makes a comedy of the confession and underscores its human naturalness. And by expressing the emotion directly, Maisie is able to grow beyond it. Her departure, by the end of the book, from both her fathers seals her release from the ambiguous oedipal embrace.

James's depiction of the oedipal drama adds a lagging affection for her stepmother to Maisie's love for her stepfather. In the book's penultimate scene, while Sir Claude's "hands went up and down gently on her shoulders," Maisie presses Mrs. Beale to give up Sir Claude: " 'I love Sir Claude—I love *him*, Maisie replied with an awkward sense that she appeared to offer it as something that would do as well [as loving Mrs. Beale]. Sir Claude had continued to pat her, and it was really an answer to his pats. 'She hates you—she hates you,' he observed with the oddest quietness to Mrs. Beale" (11:359). The neatness with which they all take their places here in a Freudian scene might seem oppressive were it not handled so delicately, and with so unerring an instinct for health. Maisie herself terminates the scene when she asks Mrs. Wix, " 'Shan't we lose the boat?' " (11:362). Her escape is so complete that even when Sir Claude fails to appear on the balcony for her as she turns around for a last look, and Mrs. Wix explains that " 'He went to *her*,' " his mistress, Mrs. Beale, Maisie's response is nothing more damaged or deprived than " 'Oh I know!' " (11:363).

Sir Claude's failure to be on the balcony to receive Maisie's parting look in one way seals the fraudulence of his affection. In another way, though, it signifies the salutary "lapse of a sequence" that enables Maisie "to recognize . . . the proof of an extinction" (11:291). The extinction is, as much as anything else, the necessary "death of her childhood" (*Prefaces*, p. 146). Thus, when Maisie and Sir Claude part, "their eyes [meet] as the eyes of those who have done for each other what they can" (11:363), that is, with a kind of serence acceptance of a natural ending. Such an extinction may seem premature, with Maisie still so young, but it represents a natural process symbolically accelerated.

The elderly, maternal governess Mrs. Wix attributes Maisie's separation from Sir Claude to her own efforts to work in the girl the triumph of what she calls "the moral sense," the last of the alien fictions in which the novel's various parent figures try to make Maisie dwell with them. Mrs. Wix presides over the genre of moral melodrama, and she herself is the melodramatic imagination of the novel personified. She thinks of Mrs. Beale as a "bad" woman (11:106), clings to didacticism for assistance in making sense of Maisie's way of bringing the story to a close, and sees all of the novel's events in simplified terms of good and evil. The beleaguered Maisie to her mind, can be saved from evil only by moral instruction. But at sea with Maisie as she is tossed from one alliance to another, the reader who may want to side with Mrs. Wix's impulse to criticize is bound to recognize that her idea of the moral sense is too simple a *vade mecum*. Marius Bewley argues that "if one denies evil in this novel one will be depriving Maisie's triumphant escape of a good deal of its significance."[7] Yet to agree that Maisie's departure from Sir Claude and Mrs. Beale is a triumph of good over evil is to reconsign the girl to a vision that is not the less melodramatic because the victimization it projects is averted. What such a vision fails to recognize is that Maisie outgrows its terms altogether as she outgrows her childhood.

Mrs. Wix's special virtue is that she is the one parental character whose emotion for Maisie is stable. Yet we respond ambivalently to the safety of her absolutely dependable affection because it is the safety of death itself in its resolution of all uncertainties. For Maisie, "she was peculiarly and soothingly safe; safer than anyone in the world, than papa, than mamma . . . safer even, though so much less beautiful, than Miss Overmore [later to become Mrs. Beale]. . . . Mrs. Wix was as safe as Clara Matilda" (11:26)—Mrs. Wix's dead daughter. That the elderly governess wears "glasses which, in humble reference to a divergent obliquity of vision, she called her straighteners" (11:25) reveals that she is walleyed, physiologically unreliable when it comes to the visual equivalent of moral rectitude. The repetitions of the word "straighteners" as a substitute for her name suggest that she is someone who strains to define ethical space, to see as straight what perhaps can never conclusively be made out to be so.

The portrait of Mrs. Wix is worth exploring further especially because she thinks and judges so much like the characters of consciousness in James's other novels. Isabel also settles her uncertainty with an allusion to the straight path, and both Fleda and Strether pride themselves on being right. James's own entertainment of uncertainty, however, constitutes one of the most important ways in which he distances himself from his figures of consciousness who are sure of their rightness. Granted that in the *Maisie* preface James employs some of the same language of salvation that he assigns to Mrs. Wix: "For satisfaction of the mind . . . the small expanding consciousness would have to be saved, have to become presentable as a register of impressions." He speaks of Maisie "sowing on barren strands, through the mere fact of presence, the seed of the moral life" (*Prefaces,* pp. 142, 143). But Mrs. Wix and James mean substantially different things by "moral life" and being "saved." As James insisted in the preface to *The Portrait,* "the 'moral' sense" in art, and, by implication, in life or in characters who represent life, depends "on the amount of felt life" experienced (*Prefaces,* p. 45). Thus, although he does indeed describe the lovers in *Maisie* as morally "barren," he says that the promise of moral life for the girl comes from her continuing "presence," not from absence, from her "register[ing] . . . impressions"—presumably including sexual impressions—not from her fleeing them.

With a tranquility very much at odds with Mrs. Wix's harried inquiries and pronouncements, Maisie arrives at a perspective on moral knowledge that endorses its importance at the same time as it treats the inclination to absolutes as something comical. The idea of moralizing experience, of seeing it as a series of lessons, is made funny.

> She judged that if her whole history, for Mrs. Wix, had been the successive stages of her knowledge, so the very climax of the concatenation would, in the same view, be the stage at which the knowledge should overflow. As she was condemned to know more and more, how could it logically stop before she should know Most? It came to her in fact . . . that she was

distinctly on the road to know Everything. She had not had
governesses for nothing. . . . She looked at the pink sky with
a placid foreboding that she soon should have learnt All.

(11:281)

Maisie's gropings after the comically capitalized quantities
"Most," "Everything," and "All" have the effect of making fun
of the pretentiousness of moral certitude—knowing everything—at the same time as they convey a feeling for the largeness of moral knowledge.

Mrs. Wix presses Maisie at the end about her knowledge
of the moral sense, like a teacher testing a slow learner on
fixed, easily specifiable facts.

> Sir Claude and Mrs. Beale stood there like visitors at an "exam."
> She had indeed [for] an instant a whiff of the faint flower [the
> moral sense] that Mrs. Wix pretended to have plucked. . . .
> Then it left her, and, as if she were sinking with a slip from
> a foothold, her arms made a short jerk. What this jerk rep-
> resented was the spasm within her of something still deeper
> than a moral sense. . . . she felt the rising of the tears she had
> kept down at the station. They had nothing—no, distinctly
> nothing—to do with her moral sense. The only thing was the
> old flat shameful schoolroom plea. "I don't know—I don't
> know."   (11:354)

Maisie substitutes for Mrs. Wix's settled convictions a knowledge that, like the early Newman's, is the larger for encompassing doubt. With her loss of a sure foothold, her admission
of uncertainty, and her openness to tears, Maisie embodies
the largest ethical appeal imagined in the novel: "something
still deeper than a moral sense."

The others, including Mrs. Wix, fend off the pain of that
moment with various rhetorical flourishes. We hear a veritable
operetta of glib voices. Mrs. Wix flares out at Sir Claude with

a florid and melodramatic didacticism: " 'You've nipped it
[Maisie's moral sense] in the bud. You've killed it when it had
begun to live' " (11:354). Later she is described as having
"found another apostrophe" (11:357). Sir Claude responds
to Mrs. Wix's accusation with a language inflated after its own
fashion, with a hushed aestheticism: " 'I've not killed anything. . . . On the contrary I think I've produced life. I don't
know what to call it . . . but, whatever it is, it's the most beautiful thing I've ever met—it's exquisite, it's sacred' " (11:354).
About Maisie's offer to give up Mrs. Wix on the condition
that he give up Mrs. Beale, Sir Claude speaks "with a relish
as intense now as if some lovely work of art or of nature had
suddenly been set down among them. He was rapidly re-
covering himself on this basis of fine appreciation" (11:356).
His ironically described "recovery" in high-tonedness, like
Mrs. Wix's immersion in moralizing, floats him away from
Maisie's wordless weeping.

Ultimately, Maisie leaves for England in the company of
Mrs. Wix. In doing so, she chooses an ending that appears
to validate conventional social values of disapproval and
judgment urged upon her by Mrs. Wix. Maisie's return to
England, however, is not an instance of fidelity to anyone else's
imagination of her life, not even Mrs. Wix's vision of her life
as moral melodrama. When the governess informs Maisie that
Sir Claude has left the balcony to keep company with his mistress and Maisie's reply is no more censorious than " 'Oh I
know!' " James notes that Mrs. Wix "still had room for wonder
at what Maisie knew" (11:363). Mrs. Wix is thus superseded
and must take her place as no more than a midwife to Maisie's
determination to give birth to herself.

As Maisie gets beyond, one after another, her father, her
mother, then Mrs. Beale and Sir Claude, and even, at last,
Mrs. Wix, she enacts a farewell to parents that has no parallel
in what James had written until that time. By showing that
Maisie's sense of the life around her has become larger than

any other character's in the book, James was suggesting that although she goes off with the elderly governess, she is actually spinning out of herself the dimensions of her experience, becoming her own source, taking custody of herself. Instead of constituting a "leak" or victimizing dissipation of power, instead of disabling her or rendering her "sterile," as James says they do Fleda (*Prefaces*, p. 131), consciousness and vision coupled with the desires of the personal self confer power on Maisie and ready her for fictions of her own. Dubious though he might have been that we can live out the designs we compose for our adult lives, James nevertheless felt that it was imperative to try to create such designs. For him, growing up was quintessentially an authorial act.

THE GOLDEN BOWL

The Golden Bowl (1904) attests to the existence of new possibilities for consciousness in James, possibilities of possessing both self and world. The novel holds together the splintered aspirations of seeing and being which vex works like *The Portrait, The Spoils, The Ambassadors,* and *The Wings of the Dove.* It shares with *What Maisie Knew* the growth of the self through silent reinvention,[8] an oedipal release, an authorial sense of relations as created and revisable structures, and the determination to include the self in these structures and thus to reconcile vision with desiring presence in the world of matter. Maggie is able to transcend the self because she can fully occupy her center. Capable of being both self and other, she is that fusion of body and eyeball that enables her to enjoy Jamesian "imagination in *predominance*."[9]

In the first volume of the novel, Maggie recapitulates earlier stages of the James character of consciousness. She appears to be a sacrificial figure, fated to lose the spoils of material experience. But in the second volume Maggie redesigns the plot of the first in an act of authorial revision similar to the ones that James performed on his own works for the New York edition. And having revised the fiction to accommodate her desiring self, she exacts her profit.

Although the young Maisie Farange ultimately takes charge of her life, she has to lose Sir Claude, the lover-father of *What Maisie Knew,* to do it. Maggie Verver, a kind of grown-up Maisie, may lose her father, but she creates and lives a fiction that includes her lover-husband. At first, however, Maggie's arrested attachment to her father Adam stands in the way of the design suggested by her marriage to Prince Amerigo. Charlotte, Maggie's friend from school and the wife of Maggie's father, explains the situation to Fanny Assingham, a friend of both couples: " 'The fact of our distinct establishments . . . makes her really see more of him than when they had the same house. To make sure she doesn't fail of it she's always arranging for it. . . . It's what I mean therefore by [my] being "placed" ' " (23:258–59). The book presents Maggie as a girl still in childhood who has not yet stopped living in her father's house despite her marriage. From his wife, Bob Assingham hears that Maggie " 'has everything there [at Eaton Square, her father's house], you know—she has clothes. . . . She has her room in his house very much as she had it before she was married' " (23:373–74). Finding Amerigo alone in Portland Place while the other couple visit together in Eaton Square, Charlotte tells the Prince that Maggie has not only monopolized her husband, but has taken her, Charlotte's, carriage for an errand, even though she has her own carriage at hand. Maggie, in effect, altogether displaces her father's wife. Her competition for her father is virtually a structural "arrangement" that "places" the leftover couple together, pressing them almost willy-nilly into resuming a love affair which, unknown to the Ververs, took place about six months before the beginning of the novel.

The severing of Maggie's oedipal tie constitutes one of the principal actions—and triumphs—of *The Golden Bowl*. James draws attention to it when he stops calling his heroine "little Maggie" and "little person," and other similar diminutives, and begins, in the second volume, and more and more as the end approaches, to refer to her as "our young woman." Samuels raises an important objection when he argues that the novel keeps undoing what it does, that its oedipal "wisdom is qualified by nostalgia for immaturity. Maggie grows up, but James's enthusiasm is less than complete."[10] Granted that there are passages toward the end of the book that Samuels, among others, justifiably questions, passages in which Maggie still yearns for her former intimacy with her father. Samuels points, for example, to the scene in which Maggie tells Fanny that she and her father are " 'lost to each other really much more than Amerigo and Charlotte are; since for them it's just, it's right, it's deserved, while for us it's only sad and strange and not caused by our fault' " (24:333). In one sense, Maggie's desire to remain close to her father throughout their lives is touching and natural. Such scenes also show James demonstrating, as he does throughout his work, how difficult it is to "grow up," how gradual and vacillating a process it is. Most important, however, these vacillations do not alter the crucial fact that Maggie ultimately refuses to let slip away from her what she values as the supreme romantic and sexual relation of her life, a relation that is available to her only as a grown woman.

Silence is the means by which Maggie accomplishes the development of a desiring self independent both of her father and Amerigo's design that she remain childlike (Amerigo promotes this design so that he can continue to align himself with Charlotte). Maggie and Amerigo "at last had silences that were almost crudities of mutual resistance" (24:60–61). In these silences, Maggie resists sexual solicitation, though at the same time she reveals an immense capacity for sexual feeling:

"She should have but to lay her head back on his shoulder with a certain movement to make it definite for him that she didn't resist. To this as they went every throb of her consciousness prompted her—every throb, that is, but one, the throb of her deeper need to know where she 'really' was" (24:57). But besides registering a resistant sexual self, Maggie is also able to make silence an instrument for encompassing reinventions that transcend resistance, and thus save her from merely defining herself negatively.

A major source of interest in this novel is, accordingly, the variety of ways it shows silence doing the emotional work of speech. One such method is the use of metaphors to give expression to fantasies of violence. Though she would not dare to articulate it in so many words, Maggie discovers in herself, through the shocking image of illegitimate motherhood, an agitated, even an overwrought self:

> She could at all events remember no time at which she had felt so excited, and certainly none . . . that so brought with it as well the necessity for concealing excitement. This birth of a new eagerness became a high pastime in her view precisely by reason of the ingenuity required for keeping the thing born out of sight. The ingenuity was thus a private and absorbing exercise, in the light of which, might I so far multiply my metaphors, I should compare her to the frightened but clinging young mother of an unlawful child. (24:7)

Because Maggie's self is represented both by the excitement or eagerness whose "birth" she seeks to conceal and by the mother who conceals it, Maggie appears to be giving birth to herself. The image of childbirth, used to suggest the bringing of forbidden emotion into the world, even if it must be kept "out of sight," signifies Maggie's authorial creation of a new self.

In another passage, Maggie imagines herself wielding a knife by means of which she may potentially either suffer or inflict a wound: "She was no longer playing with blunt and idle tools, with weapons that didn't cut. There passed across her vision ten times a day the gleam of a bare blade, and at this it was that she most shut her eyes" (24:9–10). Isabel does the same after her sole fantasy of violence against Madame Merle: "There was a moment during which, if she had turned and spoken [to Madame Merle], she would have said something that would hiss like a lash. But she closed her eyes, and then the hideous vision dropped" (4:379). The sheer number and elaborateness of the metaphor-fantasies of violence that Maggie entertains, however, establishes for them a significance and an impact in the second work that they lack in the first.

In addition to images that liberate fantasies of aggression, Maggie uses the instrument of imagined speech—words she says or hears in imagination only and are never spoken—to discharge emotions, which in James characteristically remain suppressed. This brilliant compromise, which deserves much greater critical attention than it has received, appears with unprecedented frequency and elaborateness in *The Golden Bowl* because it accomplishes what the plot demands: the expression of emotions that must be given some sort of reality in order for Maggie to reinvent herself and her fiction, but also, for success, must stop safely short of the explosive definiteness of actual speech.

One such scene occurs after Fanny shatters the golden bowl of the title, a burst of sound which itself both breaks and symbolically maintains the stillness. Fanny's intention in smashing the bowl is to preserve the strained silence surrounding Amerigo's affair with Charlotte by destroying the evidence that it exists. Amerigo enters the room at that moment, so that Fanny's crash enables Maggie, in effect, to accuse Amerigo, to let him know that she knows, without committing language to the full reach of her knowledge. In the scene that follows the crash, Maggie speechlessly gives voice both to anger and agonized pity for Amerigo, a complex range of feel-

ings it might be much more difficult for her to locate in herself
if she were to try to say them aloud.

> She wanted to say to him, "Take it [take time] . . . take all you
> need of it; arrange yourself so as to suffer least, or to be, at
> any rate, least distorted and disfigured. Only *see*, see that *I* see,
> and make up your mind on this new basis at your convenience.
> Wait—it won't be long—till you can confer again with Char-
> lotte, for you'll do it much better then—more easily to both
> of us. Above all, don't show me, till you've got it well under,
> the dreadful blur, the ravage of suspense and embarrassment
> produced, and produced by my doing, in your personal se-
> renity, your incomparable superiority." After she had squared
> her little objects on the chimney she was within an ace, in fact,
> of turning on him with that appeal. (24:184)

It is a shock at the end of this passage to be reminded that
the speech has never been spoken. It is largely because the
silences in the novel are so full of articulated emotion that
Maggie can reinvent or recompose her situation.

Fanny Assingham, Maggie's meddlesome and baroque
friend, personifies the principle of talk and, as such, provides
another alternative to dead silence. Though James does not
say so in the preface, Fanny appears to be the *ficelle* of *The
Golden Bowl.* She is the confidante with whom Maggie breaks
the silence in which she has been guarding her intensifying
conviction that Charlotte and Amerigo are lovers: " 'If I'm
helpless *and* tormented I stuff my pocket-handkerchief into
my mouth, I keep it there, for the most part, night and day,
so as not to be heard too indecently moaning. Only now, with
you, at last, I can't keep it longer; I've pulled it out and here
I am fairly screaming at you' " (24:110).

Fanny provides relief from the silent intensities bearing
down on the reader in this novel, not only in her exchanges
with Maggie, but also in those with her husband, Colonel Bob.

Fanny is a busybody. She has promoted the marriages, especially Maggie and the Prince's, and having strongly suspected Amerigo's former intimacy with Charlotte, she feels at fault for the resumption of their affair, which she surmises, and the threat it poses to the marriages. Unsympathetic at first to her wailing confidences, her husband lumbers toward her through a comic labyrinth of circumlocutions and personal pronouns without clear antecedents. "They were united for the most part but by his exhausted patience; so that indulgent despair was generally at the best his note" (24:282). But although her talk is gossip, it is gossip of a very high order. Out of the comedy of their maneuvers and the outrageousness of the language that James risks on them, there emerges a relationship that is immensely touching, something that, despite the easy way in which they are often written off, is one of the very best things in the book. Fanny's fear for the marriages and guilt over her part in the crisis she imagines may come produce an intercourse with the Colonel at once more spacious and more intimate than that of which they were capable before. Consider, for example, the collaboration imaged in the drowning-rescue metaphor that is brought indelibly to life out of the cliché "deep water":

She had been out on . . . [deep] waters for him, visibly; and his tribute to the fact had been his keeping her, even if without a word, well in sight. He hadn't quitted for an hour, during her adventure, the shore of the mystic lake; he had on the contrary stationed himself where she could signal to him at need. Her need would have arisen if the planks of her bark had parted—*then* some sort of plunge would have become his immediate duty. His present position, clearly, was that of . . . wondering if her actual mute gaze at him didn't perhaps mean that her planks *were* now parting. He held himself so ready that it was quite as if the inward man had pulled off coat and waistcoat. Before he had plunged, however—that is before he had uttered a question—he saw, not without relief, that she was making for land. . . . at last he felt her boat bump. . . . "We were all wrong. There's nothing [between Charlotte and the Prince]."

"Nothing—?" It was like giving her his hand up the bank.

(23:366)

Collaboration and intimacy take many forms in this novel. For the Assinghams by the metaphoric lake, it is a question of mutually attuned looks and signals, then of words that function for mutual assistance—"It was like giving her his hand up the bank." A moment later, Fanny's tears and an embrace become a prelude to an even greater intimacy:

He went to her and put his arm round her; he drew her head to his breast. . . . What was between them had opened out further. . . . had entered, as it were, without more words, the region of the understood. . . . And the beauty of what thus passed between them . . . with the moments of their silence, above all, which might have represented their sinking together, hand in hand for a time, into the mystic lake where he had begun, as we have hinted, by seeing her paddle alone—the beauty of it was that they now could really talk better than before. (23:378)

The collaborative intimacy of the Assinghams' embrace, which occurs close to the end of the first volume, anticipates and raises questions about the embrace on which the second volume, indeed the whole of *The Golden Bowl,* finally comes to rest, the embrace in which Maggie is held against Amerigo's breast.

Maggie's metaphoric release from her father's house is secured by one more highly significant strategy for articulating disruptive emotion safely, "humbugging." To judge by its content and its final effects, humbugging is speech that disavows itself. Thus, when Maggie humbugs her father or

Charlotte, she pretends to herself that she does not really mean the difficult truths she brings out into the open. In this way she is able to say things without guilt that are too explosive to be acknowledged in their own right. For example, under cover of pretending to herself that she is motivated by a desire to protect her father and preserve the relationships, she expresses to Adam a desire to separate from him. The novel nonetheless makes it clear that filial rebellion—a separation from her father—is precisely the emotional event she must want to occur in order to keep Amerigo.

> "Why I sacrifice you simply to everything and to everyone. I take the consequences of your marriage as perfectly natural."
> . . . "What do you call, my dear, the consequences?"
> "Your life as your marriage has made it [that is, separate from me]."
> "Well, hasn't it made it exactly what we wanted?"
> She just hesitated, then felt herself steady—oh beyond what she had dreamed. "Exactly what *I* wanted—yes." (24:269)

Maggie thus accomplishes a statement of independence from Adam by rehearsing with him a humbugged defiance that functions as a real one.

In what I take to be a corresponding scene, Maggie humbugs Charlotte. She wants Charlotte to believe that she, Maggie, is separating from her father in submission to Charlotte's desire to have Adam to herself, and so she contrives to have Charlotte accuse her of competing for Adam's time and affection, an oedipal reality that she pretends to herself is merely a polite fiction that will help Charlotte to feel triumphant. By maneuvering Charlotte into angrily casting her off and taking Adam away, she again both accomplishes and gets to feel virtuously innocent of her own necessary oedipal revolt.

> "What I ask for," Charlotte declared, "is the definite break." . . .
> . . . "You want to take my father *from* me?"

The sharp successful almost primitive wail in it made Charlotte turn, and this movement attested for the Princess the felicity of her deceit. . . .

. . . Charlotte . . . then broke into the words—Maggie had known they would come—of which she had pressed the spring. "How I see that you loathed our marriage!" (24:315–17)

James's narrative efficiency in making one character both Adam's wife and Amerigo's mistress calls attention to the process of oedipal escape. The compression by which Charlotte serves double duty serves to intensify our awareness that Maggie successfully transfers her sexual focus from father to husband. Of course the peculiarities of the novel's emotional economics are such that the oedipal conflict is fully resolved only at one end, Maggie's. Charlotte, who is approximately the same age as Maggie, is left with a husband who seems more like a father. Nevertheless, the fact that Maggie, the major figure of consciousness in the novel, is released from the attachment to her father represents a radical turn in James's conception of fictional life.

Gabriel Pearson's analysis of the novel pictures the oedipally prolonged childhood from which Maggie finally secures her release as a Freudian melodrama: "Charlotte and the Prince sometimes appear like gay, young parents, made into demons in childish imagination by their dimly divined sexual complicity." Pearson refers to the passage that conveys Maggie's sense that she is caught in a cosmic struggle between good and evil in Charlotte and Amerigo's affair: "the horror of finding evil seated all at its ease where she had only dreamed of good" (24:237). Pearson's argument, which is set forth in the single most stimulating piece of criticism I have read on the novel, is useful enough to be quoted at length. It begins with a clarifying comparison of *The Golden Bowl* and *The Turn of the Screw.*

I have always . . . read *The Turn of the Screw* as essentially a fable about the suppression of sexual identity in the Governess and its impact upon her charges. . . . The Governess . . . can no more accept that her innocents have sexual identities than she can accept sexuality in herself. What the Governess in her interrogations of Miles is asking him to confess to is nothing less than his own life's energies, most patently declared in his gender. These energies, when alienated, become demons. . . .

Charlotte and the Prince represent . . . a similar set of energies, smouldering towards explosion and experienced by Maggie as demonic and alien. . . . They are . . . embodiments of Maggie's alienated experience of her own sexuality, and of the power of possession inescapably involved in her purchase of the Prince and, as a result of her prompting, her father's of Charlotte. . . .

. . . Maggie cannot herself occupy [the] structure of civilized arrangement [constituted by the pagoda at the beginning of the second book] because it is constructed from her own alienated life. She can only enter it by entering herself and coming to some sort of terms with her power and her appetites. . . . [The action of the second book] can be seen as Maggie's entry into the pagoda and confrontation with the alien and deeply familiar forces that harbour there.[11]

Three experimental works written shortly before *The Golden Bowl* focus on the connection between alienation and the inability of the character of consciousness to exercise a predominating imagination over the materials of life. In *The Turn of the Screw*, the governess's "suppression of [her own] sexual identity" results in a world of mysteries, of endless, unanswerable questions, out of which the young woman can construct no satisfactorily predominating fiction. Bersani notes about the plot's empty center that "There is nothing to know about in *The Turn of the Screw*, there are only conjectures to be imposed." Similarly, "Fictions in *The Awkward Age* and *The Sacred Fount* don't triumph; they merely proliferate."[12] *The Awkward Age* concerns a group of voraciously speculative people who are sexually active but incapable of passion, the investment of personal emotion that lifts sexuality out of anonymity. Their obsession with analysis prevents them from desiring any turn of events enough to make it a predominating fiction. This is as true of Nanda as of the others in the sense that, although she is not frivolous, she too is alienated from her own emotional life. As she confesses to Mitchy, she loves Van theoretically—loves him precisely, that is, because her love can never be fulfilled: she " 'positively like[s] to love in vain' " (9:359). *The Sacred Fount* concerns a narrator whose failure to enter into the social and sexual world that he observes makes it impossible for him to know for certain any governing fiction of the events around him. He can speculate, chaotically, but he cannot marshall his "germs" into narrative respectability. No definitive story line emerges, and he remains a narrator capable only of alienated "imagination galore."

While Pearson's emphasis on "familiar strangeness" is appropriately Freudian in its assumptions,[13] it is necessary to see alienation metaphysically too, to grasp the full range of James's connections. Michael T. Gilmore's discussion of Maggie's innocence suggests the rich appropriateness of the metaphor of Eden to the life of consciousness in James. "History or time begins with the Fall, and one meaning of the golden bowl is that the loss of paradise—the beginning of time—is reenacted in the life of every individual. Significantly, when Maggie purchases the bowl, she places it on her mantle on the spot formerly occupied by a Louis XVI clock, as if it were itself a timepiece." Maggie's "fall" into knowledge of Amerigo and Charlotte's affair is also the beginning of her consciousness of self—her own particular identity, including, not least, her sexuality. Gilmore concludes that Maggie ultimately "accepts the burden of secular sainthood, and she learns to live in the world without being of it," achieving with Amerigo "a kind of paradise regained."[14]

At the end of the novel, Maggie's desire for Amerigo is

indeed so intense that she experiences the sense of oneness between self and world, or self and other, that reverses the dualism of ordinary alienated human consciousness which the Fall may be understood to symbolize. In this epiphanically induced paradise regained, Maggie both loses herself in the looming largeness of Amerigo's presence and locates more fully her own desiring self.

> Her desire . . . flowered in her face like a light or a darkness. . . .
>
> . . . He was so near now that she could touch him, taste him, smell him, kiss him, hold him; he almost pressed upon her, and the warmth of his face—frowning, smiling, she mightn't know which; only beautiful and strange—was bent upon her with the largeness with which objects loom in dreams. (24:352)

James's willingness to honor the mysteriousness of passion, and acknowledge the frown of deep arousal as a sort of smiling, and sexual energy as a kind of luminescence, "a light . . . darkness," like X rays or electricity made visible (as it is also in Isabel's "white lightning" kiss with Caspar Goodwood), makes *The Golden Bowl* an awesome novel of sexual intimacy.

A comparison with similar scenes in earlier works suggests the ground James has covered. In *The Spoils*, for example, this love scene occurs between Fleda and Owen:

> In a moment she had burst into sobs; in another his arms were round her; the next she had let herself go so far that even Mrs. Gereth might have seen it. He clasped her, and she gave herself—she poured out her tears on his breast. Something prisoned and pent throbbed and gushed; something deep and sweet surged up—something that came from far within and far off, that had begun with the sight of him. . . . She felt his warm lips on her face and his arms tighten with his full divination. . . . With the click of a spring, he saw. He had cleared the high wall at a bound; they were together without a veil. . . .

It was as if a whirlwind had come and gone, laying low the great false front she had built up stone by stone. The strangest thing of all was the momentary sense of desolation.

(10:188–89)

This passage anticipates the intensity of emotion in the passage from *The Golden Bowl,* and some of its rhythms suggest passionate reciprocity: "In a moment she had burst into sobs; in another his arms were round her; the next she had let herself go." Or: "He clasped her, and she gave herself." But to a very great extent, the passage dwells on dualism—separateness and the need for defenses. There is the part of Fleda that is "prisoned" and "far off," the "wall . . . built up stone by stone" between the lovers, and the sense of "desolation" and destruction caused even by its removal ("as if a whirlwind had come and gone").

For the young girl in *What Maisie Knew,* Sir Claude's "presence was like an object brought so close to her face that she couldn't see round its edges" (11:139), an epiphanic moment reminiscent of Maggie's feeling overwhelmed when Amerigo's face seems "bent upon her with the largeness with which objects loom in dreams." But the intimacy in *Maisie* that comes closest to the union of self and other, in which neither one blots out or overpowers the identity of the other, occurs between Maisie and Mrs. Wix, by dispensing with the sexual self: "Their hands were so linked and their union was so confirmed that it took the far deep note of a bell, borne to them on the summer air, to call them back to a sense of hours and proprieties. They had touched bottom and melted together" (11:289).

Maggie's desire for intimacy with Amerigo, which is the motive behind all of her actions, "the reason for what she had done," is imaged finally in a metaphor of payment,[15] which confirms the immense material profit to which consciousness has at last become heir:

She had an instant of the terror that, when there has been suspense, always precedes, on the part of the creature to be paid, the certification of the amount. Amerigo knew it, the amount. . . .

. . . His presence alone, as he paused to look at her, somehow made it the highest, and even before he had spoken she had begun to be paid in full. . . . So far as seeing that she was "paid" went he might have been holding out the money-bag for her to come and take it. (24:367–68)

Maggie "pays" by losing her father, but she does not subscribe to "the conception of paying with her life for anything she might do" (24:4). She does not believe in "paying double," like other characters of consciousness who both pay for their choices and lose through them. Thus, the purchase Maggie makes, the Prince, reimburses her, as it were. If the metaphor of payment is repugnant, it nevertheless is attached to Amerigo's "presence," his sheer being, in a way that renders a benediction on the world of matter.

James's concern with the damage done to the self by the separation of consciousness from desire is imaged perhaps most shockingly in one of his best-known later tales, published a few years after *The Golden Bowl*. In "The Jolly Corner," Spencer Brydon's self-mutilating incompleteness makes him fantasize an alter ego with two fingers grotesquely missing, "reduced to stumps, as if accidentally shot away" (17:476). The expatriate Brydon belatedly returns from Europe to a bustling New York City where he discovers "a lively stir, in a compartment of his mind never yet penetrated, of a capacity for business. . . . These virtues, so common all round him now, had been dormant in his own organism" (17:438). He has come back to look after some property that he owns, and his work on one of the houses stirs his dormant self into activity in the second, the house of his childhood, which becomes the setting for a dramatized confrontation with the repressed energies represented outside of himself by capitalism.

Alice Staverton, a friend from his past who is secretly in
love with him, contemplates his living in this now-abandoned
house, but, like Fleda when "her trouble occupied some
quarter of her soul that had closed its doors for the day and
shut out even her own sense of it" (10:234), Brydon doesn't
want to occupy the structure fully; he makes quick, fantasizing,
nighttime forays. On the last raid, he is ambushed by his
ghostly other self, whom he imagines as "evil, odious" (17:477).

The horribleness of the double and his mutilation are generally interpreted to represent what the conditions of American life, in all of its sordid materialism, would have done to
Brydon had he stayed at home. Brydon himself favors this
interpretation. To the question " 'What would it [living in
America] have made of me?' " (17:448), he answers that it
would have made him " 'Monstrous . . . hideous and offen-
sive' " (17:450). But Alice Staverton, rescuing Brydon from
the swoon into which the ghost's appearance has thrown him,
contradicts this interpretation. For her, Brydon's " 'black
stranger' " (17:483) is " 'no horror. I had accepted him. . . .
And as *I* didn't disown him, as *I* knew him . . . he must have
been, you see, less dreadful to me' " (17:484). It is Brydon's
own fear of his repressed self that gives the ghost the negative
charge that turns this into a psychological horror story. Brydon at an earlier point acknowledges that, in choosing to live
in Europe, he himself "blighted" (17:449) his dormant other.
His agency in his own blight calls to mind James's question
about Strether, apt down to the hand reference: "*Would* there
yet perhaps be time for reparation?—reparation, that is, for
the injury done his character . . . and in which he has even
himself had so clumsy a hand?" (*Prefaces,* p. 308).

Brydon is like Marcher in "The Beast in the Jungle" in being
overtaken by a sort of repressed Freudian id of a "beast" whose
"awful[ness]" (17:482) is the product—to rephrase what James
said in the essay "Matilde Serao"—of Brydon's alienation from
"himself, that is . . . [from] woman." Brydon even imagines
his situation in terms that sound borrowed from "The Beast

in the Jungle." He thinks of "stalking . . . a creature more subtle, yet at bay perhaps more formidable, than any beast of the forest," and pictures "the rear of the house . . . as the very jungle of his prey" (17:456–57, 459). James associates the ghostly beast with love and sexuality when he has Alice Staverton learn about Brydon's encounter with the ghost from the ghost himself: " 'When this morning I again saw [the ghost] I knew it would be because you had—and also . . . because you somehow wanted me. *He* seemed to tell me of that. So why . . . shouldn't I like him?' " (17:484). The story concludes, like *The Golden Bowl,* with an embrace: " 'He has a million a year,' " [Brydon] added. 'But he hasn't you.' 'And he isn't—no, he isn't—*you!*' she murmured as he drew her to his breast" (17:485).

Sicker believes that Alice Staverton's whispered reassurance—" 'And he isn't—no, he isn't—*you!*' "—means that Brydon cannot accept his ghostly other self. He argues that, with Alice's words, James cancels the effect of the embrace that follows: Brydon "resembles not so much a romantic lover as a frightened child seeking his mother's comfort after a nightmare."[16] Yet just before her whispered words, when Brydon has said to her " 'He has a million a year. . . . But he hasn't you,' " the returned expatriate has seemed to suggest a lasting romantic bond between them. It may even be his ability to make this romantic comment that triggers Alice Staverton's reassuring remark. She may be offering " 'He isn't—*you!*' " as a freeing identification in the belief that Brydon is whole now, rather than a ghostly part. And in the embrace described in the story's very last words, Brydon draws Alice Staverton to himself, rather than she, maternally, drawing him.

Psychic repression is examined and healed most fully and unequivocally, however, in *The Golden Bowl,* where the healing has the clearest implications for the life of art and the compositions of living. The scene in which Maggie allows Charlotte to assume that the departure for America is her own plan, a scene with such importance for the resolution of the oedipal drama, assists us as well in getting another "purchase" on the material of the novel; it invites us to view the novel as an aggregate of competing authorial acts by the various characters. As the scene begins, Maggie spies Charlotte escaping into the gardens from the suffocating silence of the interiors at Fawns, the Verver country house, and holding the borrowed second volume of a set to which Maggie still, by accident, has the first volume: " 'I saw you come out . . . and couldn't bear to think you should find yourself here without the beginning of your book. *This* is the beginning; you've got the wrong volume and I've brought you out the right' " (24:311). Maggie gives Charlotte the " 'right' " book, the new " 'beginning' " which she has imposed on her marriage and the plot of the novel, to replace the " 'wrong' " beginning constituted by Charlotte's affair with Amerigo and the oedipal attachment to her father of which she assists Charlotte to accuse her later in this same scene.[17]

James anchors our understanding of *The Golden Bowl* as a competition among its characters for supreme imaginative command of the novel in the characters' relations with a Bloomsbury merchant whose shop contains the golden bowl of the title. While looking for a gift for Maggie on the eve of the marriage, Amerigo and Charlotte find themselves in this shop, whose owner, a "master . . . devoted to his business" (23:104), shows them a golden bowl, which James spells in capital letters: "The dealer . . . turn[ed] straightway toward a receptacle to which he hadn't yet resorted and from which, after unlocking it, he extracted a square box. . . . [He] removed from its nest a drinking-vessel larger than a common cup. . . . He handled it with tenderness, with ceremony. . . . 'My Golden Bowl,' he observed—and it sounded on his lips as if it said everything" (23:112). Charlotte realizes later that

> She had . . . found their *antiquario* interesting; partly because he cared so for his things, and partly because he cared—well,

so for *them*. "He likes his things—he loves them," she was to say; "and it isn't only—it isn't perhaps even at all—that he loves to sell them. I think he would love to keep them if he could; and he prefers at any rate to sell them to right people. We, clearly, were right people . . . and that's why . . . you could make out, or at least I could, that he cared for us. (23:106)

The shopkeeper is cast in the likeness of James as he was to represent himself in the *Portrait* preface four years later:

> The figure [the "germ" of a work] has . . . *been* placed— placed in the imagination that detains it, preserves, protects, enjoys it, conscious of its presence in the dusky, crowded, heterogeneous back-shop of the mind very much as a wary dealer in precious odds and ends . . . is conscious of the rare little "piece" left in deposit . . . which is already there to disclose its merit afresh as soon as a key shall have clicked in a cupboard door.
>
> . . . [I] recall . . . my pious desire but to place my treasure right. I quite remind myself thus of the dealer resigned not to "realise," resigned to keeping the precious object locked up indefinitely rather than commit it, at no matter what price, to vulgar hands. For there *are* dealers in these forms and figures and treasures capable of that refinement. (*Prefaces*, pp. 47–48)

In the preface to *The Golden Bowl* itself, James speaks of Alvin Langdon Coburn's photographic illustration for the first volume of the novel, which was to be "a view of the small shop in which the Bowl is first encountered," as a concrete representation of "a shop of the mind, of the author's projected world" (*Prefaces*, p. 334). And he might be said to have glossed his appearance in the novel with an almost comical exactitude when he wrote "I get down into the arena and do my best to live and breathe and rub shoulders and converse with the persons engaged in the struggle that provides for the others in the circling tiers the entertainment of the great game" (*Prefaces*, p. 328).

James's preoccupation with placing his "treasure," which is the shopkeeper's concern with selling the gilt cup to "right people," generates a number of scenes in which the authorial dealer "rubs shoulders and converses with the persons engaged in the struggle," offering them "My Golden Bowl," the book not less than the object. In the first volume, he offers it to Amerigo and Charlotte who do not buy it, and then, in the second volume, to Maggie who does. James launches his material in the person of the shady merchant, offering the book and the invention of its plot to whichever character is willing to "pay" for it.

Perhaps because it is the last in the series of prefaces he wrote in revising his works for the New York edition, over half of the preface to *The Golden Bowl* focuses on the act of revision and what it means:

> To revise is to see, or to look over, again. . . . I had attached to it, in a brooding spirit, the idea of re-writing—with which it was to have in the event . . . almost nothing in common. . . . On the other hand the act of revision, the act of seeing it again, caused whatever I looked at on any page to flower before me as into the only terms that honourably expressed it . . . the particular vision of the matter itself that experience had at last made the only possible one. (*Prefaces*, pp. 338–39)

Among all of James's completed works the proto-modernist *Golden Bowl* is the most self-conscious about its aesthetic aims and processes. James's interest in revision, in competitive visions of the same material, is enacted as a feature of the novel's plot when he makes every one of the six principals an aspiring author of the situation.

Fanny's hyperactive imagination produces flagrant aberrations of the plot. She projects back in time, before the opening of the novel, for instance, and invents a new line of exposition for Charlotte and Amerigo's romance, in which though " 'they were thoroughly in love,' " they were not lovers because, as Fanny imagines it, " 'there wasn't time' " (23:71). She designs a plot for an altogether different novel, one in which her husband would be in love with Maggie: "The Colonel's confessed attention had been enlisted . . . as never yet . . . but this, she could assure him she perfectly knew, was not a bit because he was sorry for her . . . but because when once they had been opened he couldn't keep his eyes from resting complacently, resting almost intelligently, on the Princess. If he was in love with *her* now" (24:122).

Fanny the matchmaker is Fanny composing, Fanny authorial. James shows Amerigo thinking that Fanny "had *made* his marriage" (23:21); it had been "her design" (23:21); she had " 'had the conception' " of it (23:28). Fanny invents Charlotte's marriage, too, lest Charlotte continue to be "a piece of waste and a piece of threatened failure" in the plot of their lives (23:389). She confides to the Colonel in a burst of authorial enthusiasm:

> "We're to marry her [Charlotte]. . . . It will make up. . . . If I made a mistake."
> "You'll make up for it by making another? . . . if we can but strike so wild why keep meddling?"
> . . . "Where would you have been, my dear, if I hadn't meddled with *you?*"
> "Ah, that wasn't meddling—I was your own . . . from the moment I didn't object."
> "Well, these people won't object. *They* are my own too."
> (23:85–86)

Fanny, like Aunt Penniman in *Washington Square,* is unable, except when composing with her husband, to foster a design legitimated by personal emotion. Her acts of authorial possession are merely "meddling." Only Maggie's designs for all of them wed personal emotion to authorial style, sincerity to artfulness, thereby giving them an unprecedented power and legitimacy.

The Colonel, for his part, accuses his wife of being in love with the Prince, a fiction with a small measure of truth: " 'What happened . . . was that you fell violently in love with the Prince yourself. . . . *You* couldn't marry him, any more than Charlotte could—that is not to yourself. But you could to . . . your little friend [Maggie]' " (23:81). In addition, the Colonel dedicates his authorial energies to the task of revising not only his wife's speech, but her proliferating plots: " 'If we can but strike so wild, why keep meddling?' " James explains, "He edited for their general economy the play of . . . [Fanny's] mind, just as he edited, savingly, with the stump of a pencil, her redundant telegrams" (23:67). It is not only that Fanny's scenarios have little to do with the "reality" of the novel, but that they introduce an irresponsible superfluity of plot, more than the novel could possibly use.

Fanny's downfall as the novel's most hyperactive imaginer is due precisely to her frivolity, her failure to balance the aesthetic pleasure of design with personal accountability, to assume any responsibility for the outcome of her compositions. " 'They were making a mess of such charming material. . . . I always pay for it, sooner or later, my sociable, my damnable, my unnecessary interest' " (23:388–89). The reality, however, is that Fanny is not at all eager to "pay" and, in fact, is unwilling, like the spectatorial Ralph Touchett, to sustain the "bleeding participants" through the combat. Instead, she is only too happy to let Maggie " 'see me somehow through! . . . She'll carry the whole weight of us' " (23:381).

A turning point that signals Fanny's unsuitability for authorial offices occurs when she coins a phrase with the Colonel for dispensing altogether with the adultery that her matchmaking mania has promoted. She is under the illusion that it is possible to perform the ultimate revision on time and events—a cancellation: "What was the basis, which Fanny absolutely exacted [for midnight talks with her husband], but that Charlotte and the Prince must be saved—so far as con-

sistently speaking of them as still safe might save them?"
(23:378). Fanny elaborates on this fiction of "still safe" when
she assures the Colonel that " 'Nothing—in spite of everything—*will* happen. Nothing *has* happened. Nothing *is* happening' " (23:400). This is the gainsaying fiction that Fanny
seeks to protect when she smashes the golden bowl: she
"dashed it boldly to the ground. . . . After which, 'Whatever
you [Maggie] meant by it—and I don't want to know *now*—
has ceased to exist' " (24:179).

Maggie also wants to cancel the past, once she discovers
that Charlotte and Amerigo have been intimate, but "she
[shakes] her head as against all easy glosses" (24:178) of the
text she reads with Fanny. Yeazell argues that Maggie and
Fanny in essence make the same kind of authorial effort.[18]
But while Maggie, like Fanny, wants the perfection of " 'the
golden bowl—as it *was* to have been . . . the bowl without the
crack' " (24:216–17), her remedy differs radically from that
of Fanny who, as a result of the inadequacy of her solution,
is virtually squeezed out of the last part of the book. Maggie's
difference is that ultimately she is willing to pay for the direction in which her design pushes the plot, while Amerigo,
Charlotte, and Fanny have assumed authorial powers without
consenting to be accountable.

The lovers have a chance to impose their vision permanently
on the book's course when James, in the guise of the Bloomsbury shopkeeper, gives them the opportunity to buy his gold-
en bowl, but neither one of them wants to "pay" for it. The
bowl has a crack, a flaw, whose visibility is concealed by the
gilding of the crystal. Amerigo sees this more quickly and
surely than Charlotte:

> "You mean you really don't know . . . what's the matter with
> it? . . ."
> . . . "How could *you* see—out in the street!"
> "I saw before I went out. It was because I saw that I did go

out. I didn't want to have another scene with you before that rascal. . . ."

"Is he a rascal?" Charlotte asked. . . .

". . . I saw the object itself. It told its story. No wonder it's cheap."

"But it's exquisite," Charlotte, as if with an interest in it now made even tenderer and stranger, found herself moved to insist. (23:118–19)

Amerigo's observation that the bowl has a crack prevents him from wanting to buy it, although by purchasing it, "paying" for it, he could perhaps give "the story" of their love affair, symbolized in part by the crack, the status of an enduring plot for the novel.

In the midst of all the verbs of seeing and knowing on which he leans for Amerigo's advantage in this scene, James nevertheless celebrates a superior capacity for complexity in Charlotte. Holland suggests that "The Prince's reaction to the bowl, accompanied by his departure from Charlotte's side and from the shop, is distinctly correct but crudely simple in view of the moral complexities which Charlotte explores while bargaining with the shopkeeper."[19] Although his refusal to accept the flawed bowl perhaps adumbrates his ability to be "saved" by Maggie at the end of the novel, Amerigo is a less genuinely moral character than Charlotte in the sense that morality, for James, depended upon "the amount of felt life" (*Prefaces,* p. 45) to which consciousness makes itself heir. Amerigo explains to Fanny on the eve of his marriage,

" 'I've of course something that in our poor dear backward old Rome sufficiently passes for it [the moral sense]. But it's no more like yours than the tortuous stone staircase—half-ruined into the bargain!—in some castle of our *quattrocento* is like the 'lightning elevator' in one of Mr. Verver's fifteen-storey buildings. Your moral sense works by steam—it sends you up like a rocket. Ours is slow and steep and unlighted, with so many of the steps missing that—well, that it's as short in almost any case to turn round and come down again.' " (23:31)

The moral ideal implicit in this passage is something between the facile and mechanically sure "lightning elevator" and the virtually unnegotiable staircase. It is just the *process* of ascending, a journey Charlotte is at least willing to begin to undertake. Readers also are required to undertake this confusing journey in the course of the book, to surrender, like Charlotte, to the shopkeeper's dubious logic, even though they will probably end up in the same place as Amerigo (who got there, however, by never leaving it).

Charlotte is an adventurer in the largest sense of the word. She is willing to deal with uncertainty and imperfection; even, possibly, to be defrauded. In this respect she is like James when he has the courage to acknowledge: "Strangely fertilizing, in the long run, does a wasted effort of attention often prove. It all depends on *how* the attention has been cheated" (*Prefaces*, pp. 41–42). And in "The Lesson of Balzac," James avers that "it is in . . . *waste* . . . the waste of time, of passion, of curiosity, of contact—that true initiation resides."[20] Charlotte's greater capacity for the burden of complexity does not make her irreproachable; nor does it save her from the error of simplifying Maggie in the end. But it does enable her, after Amerigo leaves the Bloomsbury shop, to engage the dealer in talk that allows us to contemplate the novel's most trying moral discriminations.

> "I've had it [the bowl] a long time without selling it. I think I must have been keeping it, madam, for you."
> "You've kept it for me because you've thought I mightn't see what's the matter with it?"
> . . . "What *is* the matter with it?"
> "Oh it's not for me to say; it's for you honestly to tell me. Of course I know something must be."

"But if it's something you can't find out isn't that as good as if it were nothing?" (23:114)

Essentially the dealer asks: Does the crack matter if you don't know it is there? Despite the obvious oiliness of the question, it is not intended that the answer be easy to come by. The possibility that the dealer's questions are unmitigatedly rotten and the dealer himself corrupt, a charlatan, is inseparable from the conceivably valid view, which Charlotte recognizes demands "justice" (23:117), that there is "as good" as nothing wrong if nothing can be discovered to be wrong. In addition, as Charlotte seems to feel when she is drawn to the bowl even more once she discovers that it is flawed, there is the chance that perfection is unimportant—an unrealistic, unavailing, and possibly even harmful demand to make of beauty, art, and human experience.

Yet although Charlotte appreciates and wants the bowl, imperfection and all, she, like Amerigo, foregoes the purchase. Like Strether when he is confronted by the painting of life on the river, she feels she cannot afford it. Charlotte and Amerigo's purchase of the bowl would mean, projectively, that they were willing to take their composition of the plot seriously, that is, to its logical conclusion. Ultimately that would mean nothing less than the complete undoing of both marriages. Charlotte and Amerigo did not marry each other when they had the chance because both of them were poor, and the breakup of the marriages would merely put them back in the same untenable position. Their determination to stay married helps make it possible for Maggie to recompose their situation.

In the first half of the novel, Maggie and Adam, like Charlotte and Amerigo, are living certain fictions without having paid for the right to do so: "That purchased social ease, the sense of the comfort and credit of their house [obtained when Charlotte and Amerigo perform their social functions for them] . . . had essentially the perfection of something paid for, but . . . 'came' on the whole so cheap that it might have been felt as costing—as costing the parent and child—nothing" (24:47). Through Maggie's memory and narration, the Bloomsbury shopkeeper makes a second appearance in the novel, in volume 2, once again to offer the golden bowl for sale, with the attendant rights and responsibilities of authorship. This time, Maggie herself makes the purchase, and begins to "pay" for the marital compositions that she and her father have chosen. The dealer's importance here and earlier in the novel has been discussed too little.

Amerigo recalls, over the pieces of Maggie's purchase shattered by Fanny,

> "The man . . . wanted awfully to work off his bowl. But I didn't believe in it and we didn't take it."
> . . . "I did 'believe in it,' you see—must have believed in it somehow instinctively; for I took it as soon as I saw it. . . ."
> . . . "But shall you at least get your money back?"
> "Oh I'm far from wanting it back—I feel so that I'm getting its worth." (24:194–95, 198)

Like Charlotte, Maggie is willing to take the chance of being cheated. The shopkeeper, however, moved by a guilty conscience, visits Maggie to apologize and offer to return the money.

> He hadn't liked what he had done and what he had above all made such a "good thing" of having done [selling the flawed bowl to Maggie as a gift for her father]. . . . the partner of her bargain had yearned to see her again. . . .
> It was after this that the most extraordinary incident of all of course had occurred—his pointing to the two photographs [photographs of Amerigo and Charlotte set on the mantle] with the remark that those were persons he knew. . . . And he had spoken . . . for that conviction of the nature and degree of their intimacy under which, in spite of precautions, they

hadn't been able to help leaving him. . . . He had been sure they were great people, but no, ah no, distinctly, hadn't "liked" them as he liked the Signora Principessa. (24:223–25)

Before the dealer reappears, the lovers' affair is made vulnerable to judgment only by Maggie's suffering. That is, the affair can be criticized only, paradoxically, by validating the assumptions behind the dealer's oily question—there is something wrong only because Maggie's knowledge or at least suspicion has begun to make it wrong. For as James has managed it, Charlotte and Amerigo are virtually compelled to renew their intimacy by the pressure of Maggie and Adam's arrangements, which bring them constantly together, without the company of their spouses, to act as a kind of composite household for the view of the world. The alliance that is forced upon them, the roles that they are required to enact in the token household they are expected to form, seem virtually to say that Charlotte and Amerigo are a couple. From one perspective, then, they seem to be cooperating with the Ververs' designs by resuming the affair, and that makes it difficult to blame them.

But the vendor's reappearance definitively changes the way in which we regard the affair symbolized by the crack that the dealer himself now regards so guiltily. His guilty conscience creates a retrospective eye of judgment through which we see the affair as inherently dubious. His apparently reformed moral sense has the effect of calling Charlotte and Amerigo into question retroactively. Even though they have not done business with him, they have conducted their affair in a way that coincides with the assumptions behind his early question: " 'If it's something you can't find out, isn't that as good as if it were nothing?' " This is also, of course, the assumption behind Fanny's resolve to protect Maggie by destroying the evidence—the bowl—as it is a major source of *her* moral obliquity. James protects Fanny's status in the first volume, as he protects Charlotte and Amerigo's, so that the reader can have the experience of ascending that half-ruined staircase of the *quattrocento*. He protects them all from what he disparages as

> the so-called "moral" eagerness. The English writer wants to make sure, first of all, of your moral judgment; the French is willing, while it waits a little, to risk, for the sake of his subject and its interest, your spiritual salvation. Madame Marneffe [in Balzac's *Les Parents Pauvres*], detrimental, fatal as she is, is "exposed," so far as anything in life, or in art, may be, by the working-out of the situation and the subject themselves.[21]

Only with the merchant's second appearance does the novel furnish means for evaluating with any assurance the positions of Fanny, Charlotte, Amerigo, and the shopkeeper himself.

The dealer's preference for Maggie is James's recognition of her, among his four eligible "great" characters, as the one who is singularly equipped to be "the partner of . . . [his] bargain." "She brought them [the pieces] over to the chimney-piece, to the conspicuous place occupied by the cup before Fanny's appropriation of it. . . . There was . . . nothing to hold them but Maggie's hands" (24:182–83). That Maggie believed in the bowl enough to buy it when Amerigo and Charlotte passed it up, and that she is willing to hold together the fragments of the bowl for which Fanny refuses accountability even though she has "appropriated" it, means that Maggie is entitled to compose *The Golden Bowl* as she wants it to be. Just as her hands hold together the fragments of the bowl on the mantle, her accountability for the novel's relationships and plot forestalls the impending disintegration both of the marriages and the narrative. She saves the various forms in a supreme exercise of the imagination that the other characters feel they cannot afford.

In earlier James, payment meant what characters felt they

had to put down for a mistake, an erroneous composition of their experience, but paying did not entitle them to correct the mistake or revise their lines of intention. Isabel tells Henrietta in response to the latter's suggestion that she correct the mistake of her marriage by leaving it: " 'I can't publish my mistake. . . . One must accept one's deeds' " (4:284). Strether advises little Bilham, " 'Live all you can; it's a mistake not to' " (21:217), but feels that it is too late for him to revise that mistake, and that he can only accept the prospect of responsible payment. Both Isabel and Strether pay first in what they lose and again in what they keep, because what they keep, or return to, lacks clear revision. For Maggie, however, revision makes a discernible, lived difference; her "re-perusal" is visibly "registered" (*Prefaces*, p. 339). In *The Golden Bowl*, payment *is* authorship. Although Maggie's actions preserve the form of marriage (two marriages, in fact), so that she too, like Isabel, "accepts her deed," "paying" for her marriage as she purchases the golden bowl, bowl and book, entitles her to revise its mistakes.

This capacity for revision opens up new ways of understanding the preservation of the social surface with which most of James's novels end. Isabel preserves her marriage rather than eloping with Caspar or living eccentrically alone like Mrs. Touchett; Fleda insists that Owen honor his pledge to Mona even though there may be little love on either side; Strether, despite disavowal of his mission, correctly preserves ambassadorial form by returning to America, as though to report to his head of state; and Maisie returns to Mrs. Wix, official guardian of the socially sanctioned moral sense, rather than live with the lovers. Yet, although James's sense of an ending usually coincides with the conventions prescribed by social forms, that does not mean that he fully endorses those conventions.

To be *seen* to be new, even new fictions must exist in the context of previous compositions. New forms exist not in a vacuum, but by virtue of earlier demarcations and definitions whose boundaries they challenge, push off from, extend, remake. The difficulty is deciding when old forms or fictions have undergone sufficient activity to become new, when revision is indeed not merely rewriting, but an "act of seeing . . . again" (*Prefaces*, p. 339). Isabel's portrait, for example, is bound within the frame of the predictable imposed by Osmond's small range of response to her gestures. She may try new gestures, but they will be contained within his house of fiction, which gives the character of resistance to all of her new moves. Maggie also preserves the inherited forms; she protects the conventional configuration of married life for two sets of couples against all subversive challenges. But while Isabel, Fleda, and Strether appear to find little for themselves in the forms they observe, Maggie and Maisie manage to derive from them a sense of personal satisfaction. In thus personalizing the forms they inherit, they make them new.

In suggesting that limits, containers, and inherited forms are extremely important to James's fiction, Poirier identifies a series of shadow forms, or what we might call "moulds," behind James's early novels—works by other authors against which James exercised in writing his own. Poirier proposes that Hawthorne's work lies behind *Roderick Hudson* and *The American*, that Balzac's work lies behind *Washington Square*, that Jane Austen's lies behind *The Europeans*, George Eliot's behind *The Portrait*, and Dickens's behind *The Bostonians*.[22] Yet James's efforts do not strike readers primarily as negations of other authors' efforts. They read what James wrote because he got beyond resistance. Such an ability substantially to transform and move beyond the earlier form sets apart the genuine reinventions from the false or partial ones in which most of James's main characters get caught resisting. Honoring the inherited forms constitutes a genuinely new act for Maggie because she has transformed the emotional content of payment. Departing from the oedipal house of fiction, her sexuality and imagination are released together.

Maggie buys The Golden Bowl, holds it together, takes its composition in hand, contributes her own presence to the design, and proceeds to enjoy her profit—earning for herself the right to think of the bowl possessively as "her golden bowl" (24:236). Equally important, though, she also performs the kind of literary self-transcendence that James praised in Balzac when he said the French author "liked . . . to get into the constituted consciousness, into all the clothes, gloves and whatever else, into the very skin and bones, of the habited, featured, colored, articulated form of life that he desired to present."[23] Her intensity of self-implication with the novel's other characters is so great, in fact, that she virtually breathes with them in their pain. This is convincing precisely because consciousness for Maggie increasingly becomes the instrument of a desiring self. Because its use as an instrument for feeling what others feel has ceased to be substitutive, as it is with Isabel and Fleda, it acquires an authority and a weight far beyond what it had with them.

Maggie's capacity for embracing the characters and situations that constitute the novel includes the facility already noted for imagining unspoken speech. This facility ultimately involves words that are uttered not only in her imagination, but, attributively, in others'. For example, she imagines Amerigo silently pleading with her: " 'Leave me my reserve; don't question it—it's all I have just now, don't you see? . . . I promise you something or other, grown under cover of it, even though I don't yet quite make out what.' . . . She had turned away from him with some such unspoken words as that in her ear. . . . she had spiritually heard them" (24:221). Like a floating transparent eyeball, Maggie can even imagine gestures and speech in situations at which she is not present. She

> saw [Charlotte], face to face with the Prince, take from him the chill of his stiffest admonition. . . . She heard her ask . . .

what tone, in God's name—since her bravery didn't suit him—
she *was* then to adopt; and, by way of a fantastic flight of di-
vination she heard Amerigo reply. . . . She breathed Charlotte's
cold air—turned away from him in it with her, turned with
her, in growing compassion, this way and that. (24:282)

The intimacy of Maggie's identification with the other characters is so great that at times it becomes visceral, and she
seems to share with them the same body:

> Something indubitably had come up for [Charlotte]. . . . it
> represented a new complication and had begotten a new anx-
> iety—things these that she carried about with her done up in
> the napkin of her lover's accepted rebuke while she vainly
> hunted for some corner where she might put them safely
> down. The disguised solemnity, the prolonged futility of the
> search . . . there were moments while she watched with her,
> thus unseen, when the mere effect of being near her was to
> feel her own heart in her throat. (24:284)

Scenes like this are given no independent existence or veri-
fication outside of Maggie's imagination, but they do not seem
to need it, which is a tribute to her authorial power. She is
put in the position of having what she imagines *become* the
novel. Thus even the shopkeeper's appearance in the second
volume occurs not as an event in its own right, as it did in
the first, but through Maggie's recreation of the scene.

James takes the greatest risks with his material when acts
of possession come uncomfortably close to being acts of tyranny. To "discipline" the material is to insist on the centrality
of the heretofore transcendent self. The scenes of apparent
tyranny are so difficult to assess because they merely carry to
their logical extreme the impulses for profitable possession
and authorial command whose realization by a character of

consciousness is perhaps, in the long view, the novel's greatest achievement. It is doubtful that these scenes can ultimately be settled, critically speaking, or that James meant them to be.

Paradoxically, the evidence that self-possession and tyranny have drawn perilously close together comes, for the most part, through Maggie's self-transcendent flights of empathy with other characters since it is these moments which make palpable the anguish that Maggie's recomposition is causing. Pearson finds Maggie's empathic imaginings "impertinent," an "exercise of power and control."[24] To save it from being impertinent manipulation, empathic imagining would have to become collaborative. That is, Maggie's empathic knowledge of the pain she is causing would have to create a willingness to share her command of the fiction, something that does not really happen. Philip M. Weinstein notes "something appalling in the uncritical use of the author's relation to his characters as a model for Maggie's relation to her family."[25] That such use was not, in fact, "uncritical," and that reservations of this kind were also James's own, seems evident from the sinister edge occasionally imparted to Maggie's exercise of authorial power, as it is imparted to Osmond's in *The Portrait.* Maggie, at different times in the novel, is Isabel, deceived and manipulated, and Osmond, controlling, a collector, and the artist of the fiction. Just as Isabel becomes Osmond's *Portrait,* the marriage with Amerigo becomes Maggie's *Bowl.* Each of them takes command of the book's material and its title. The reservations with which James imbues such command represent his ambivalence toward all acts of supreme authorship, his own included.

Maggie explains her strategy toward the adulterous couple, a kind of loving ruthlessness, to a suspicious Fanny in this way:

> "They move at any rate among the dangers I speak of— between that of their doing too much and that of their not

having any longer the confidence or the nerve . . . to do
enough. . . . And that's how I make them do what I like!"
. . . "You're terrible."
Maggie thoughtfully shook her head. "No; I'm not terrible. . . . I *am* mild. I can bear anything. . . . For love." . . .
. . . "Is that what you call it when you make them, for terror
as you say, do as you like?"
"Ah there wouldn't be any terror for them if they had nothing to hide." (24:115–16)

James demonstrates here the immense cruelties that can grow
out of intending kindness.

The "awful mixture" (24:292) of love and cruelty by means
of which Maggie controls Charlotte and Amerigo emerges
most disturbingly when she "translates" their pain, and thus
accepts the text. Charlotte

stopped when her husband stopped . . . and the likeness of
their connexion wouldn't have been wrongly figured if he had
been thought of as holding in one of his pocketed hands the
end of a long silken halter looped round her beautiful neck. . . .
Maggie's translation of it . . . came out . . . "Yes, you see—I
lead her now by the neck, I lead her to her doom, and she
doesn't so much as know what it is, though she has a fear in
her heart which, if you had the chances to apply your ear there
that I, as a husband, have, you would hear thump and thump
and thump." (24:287–88)

Imagining Amerigo in their London home, Maggie "saw him
. . . wander in the closed dusky rooms from place to place or
else for long periods recline on deep sofas and stare before
him through the smoke of ceaseless cigarettes. . . . It all came
to her there [at Fawns]—he got off to escape from a sound
. . . that of Charlotte's high coerced quaver before the cabinets

in the hushed gallery" (24:293–94). This is the unvoiced "shriek of a soul in pain" (24:292) that Maggie imagines she hears as Charlotte guides visitors through her husband's collection. And at the end of the novel, Maggie thinks of asking Amerigo to give Charlotte some memorable word or gesture to take with her to America, "some benefit that might be carried away into exile like the last saved object of price of the *émigré,* the jewel wrapped in a piece of old silk and negotiable some day in the market of misery" (24:330).

For sheer horror, nothing elsewhere in James can match these passages. They unleash a language of pain so overpowering that one wants to cry "Stop." There is no real place in the book for what this voice says; the only response to it would be a different book, different from the one Maggie makes. Maggie even posits a theory of the necessity of Charlotte's suffering for her own and the Prince's new start: " 'It's as if her unhappiness had been necessary to us—as if we had needed her, at her own cost, to build us up and start us' " (24:346). The theory may salve our distress at the immensity of pain by converting what would otherwise be waste into potential for good, but it also renews our apprehensions since there is probably no use that ought to profit from such pain.

Charlotte's way of bearing pain enhances her value as a magnificent presence in Maggie and Adam's eyes. In their last, much-quoted conversation, Maggie and Adam fall to taking inventory, cataloguing Charlotte and Amerigo as "high expressions of the kind of human furniture required aesthetically by such a scene. . . . Their companions . . . [sat] as still, to be thus appraised, as a pair of effigies of the contemporary great on one of the platforms of Madame Tussaud" (24:360–61). Collecting people is an activity analogous to possessing them as material for fiction. In either case, there is the danger of ending up with wax "effigies."

Maggie and Adam see each other also as collectors' items.

Maggie, for instance, sees Adam's face inside the frame of an early Florentine religious painting he gave her when she married:

> The tenderness represented for her by his sacrifice of such a treasure had become to her sense a part of the whole infusion, of the immortal expression; the beauty of his sentiment looked out at her always, from the beauty of the rest, as if the frame made positively a window for his spiritual face: she might have said to herself at this moment that in leaving the thing behind him, held as in her clasping arms, he was doing the most possible toward leaving her a part of his palpable self. (24:359)

The virtually religious generosity represented by the gift of the painting transforms it. A comparison of the two passages, the one in which Maggie turns Adam into a painting and the other in which Maggie and Adam turn the lovers into objects of value, helps make clear why scenes like the latter throughout the book have disturbed many readers. Maggie and her father make each other into art, which reminds them of the human reality and recalls them to it. Adam's painting brings Maggie back to his "palpable self." The lovers, however, are objectified by the aesthetic eye, turned into nonhuman entities. This scants the human claims that the novel's language of pain teaches us to value.

A distinction ought to be drawn, however, between Adam's attitude toward human collections and Maggie's. Adam seems to regard his wife principally in entrepreneurial terms; she will be the cicerone in his American museum, and also the prime exhibit. He sees the Prince as " 'a part of his collection . . . a *morceau de musée*' " (23:12). Though Maggie also sees Amerigo and Charlotte as museum pieces, this is not the full extent of her vision. She desires a design capable of wedding the aesthetic motive with the motive of passion, and the fiction she invents is large enough and different enough from Adam's to do this. The house of fiction from which she departs is, among other ways of thinking about it, Adam's conception of marriage as a passionless patron-and-museum-piece arrangement.[26]

Adam's one passion, apparently, is "the passion for perfection at any price" (23:146). His optimism about the artful perfectibility of life, and the desirability of that perfection, which encompasses so much less than Maggie's, results in a mincing trepidation before "the wilderness of mere mistakes" (23:143), and a huckstering papal grandiosity. His plan to build a magnificent art museum in American City is "positively civilization condensed, concrete, consummate, set down by his hands as a house on a rock—a house from whose open doors and windows, open to grateful, to thirsty millions, the higher, the highest knowledge would shine out to bless the land" (23:145). In the prefaces, James infuses discussions of his art with religious language to register the sacredness for him of the aesthetic undertaking, but his language is free of the messianic delusions of grandeur and salesman pitch—"grateful . . . thirsty millions"—which comically blight the integrity of Adam's mission. James's "passion for perfection" is pursued in a different spirit, a spirit that honors those "lurking forces of expansion . . . necessities of upspringing in the seed" (*Prefaces,* p. 42), even at the risk of error. Maggie, however, although she accepts the bowl's imperfection and the mistakes it embodies, yearns ultimately, like Adam, to have it perfect: " 'the golden bowl—as it *was* to have been . . . The bowl without the crack' " (24:216–17). She remains her father's daughter to the extent that she promotes her perfecting version of the relations so effectively that she locks up the plot in her own house of fiction. We are to take Maggie's solution as final, I think, not reinventible.

Collaborative experience, which escapes the potential melodrama of both tyranny and self-sacrifice, has been the hallmark of Charlotte and Amerigo's relation.

"It's sacred," he said at last.

"It's sacred," she breathed back at him. They vowed it, gave it out and took it in, drawn, by their intensity, more closely together. Then of a sudden, through this tightened circle . . . everything broke up, broke down, gave way, melted and mingled. Their lips sought their lips, their pressure their response and their response their pressure. (23:312)

They echo each other and are returned to themselves: " 'It's sacred,' she breathed back at him." James's language reflects a movement toward supremely collaborative love-making. There is the passage from short, punctuated clauses with clear subject/verb structure, to long floating groups of words undefined by grammatical structuring or marks of punctuation, the verbal equivalent of "melted and mingled"—"their pressure their response and their response their pressure." Subject and object become interchangeable in these reciprocally inverted phrases which are given definition only by the shared pronoun "their."

At Matcham, before he and Charlotte depart for Gloucester, Amerigo contemplates their

identities of impulse—they had had them repeatedly before; and if such unarranged but unerring encounters gave the measure of the degree in which people were, in the common phrase, meant for each other, no union in the world had ever been more sweetened with rightness. . . . Something in her long look at him now out of the old grey window, something in the very poise of her hat, the colour of her necktie, the prolonged stillness of her smile, touched into sudden light for him all the wealth of the fact that he could count on her. He had his hand there, to pluck it, on the open bloom of the day; but what did the bright minute mean but that her answering hand was already intelligently out? So therefore while the minute lasted it passed between them that their cup was full; which cup their very eyes, holding it fast, carried and steadied and began, as they tasted it, to praise. (23:356)

She came toward him in silence while he moved to meet her;
the great scale of this particular front, at Matcham, multiplied
thus, in the golden morning, the stages of their meeting and
the successions of their consciousness. (23:358)

Ordinary realistic details—"the old grey window . . . the very
poise of her [Charlotte's] hat, the colour of her necktie, the
prolonged stillness of her smile," "the great scale of . . .
[Matcham's] front"—are radiant with meaning. For Amerigo
they epiphanically "touch . . . into sudden light" the sense that
"he could count on her." Charlotte and Amerigo have a sense
of greater meaning in the scene both separately and together,
and, more exactly, because they are together: "He had his
hand there. . . . but what did the bright minute mean but that
her answering hand was already intelligently out?" Their collaboration rises to a devotional pitch: "Their very eyes . . .
began, as they tasted it, to praise." Epiphanies are triggered
in each by the presence of the other. The "multiplied . . . stages
of their meeting and the successions of their consciousness"
apparently constitute for both an effect like the sense of in-
finity created by double mirrors set up facing each other. And
in the infinitely "multiplied . . . stages of their meeting," time
is drawn out in a present moment that seems to go on forever:
paradise regained.[27]

To be sure, James sounds an early note of caution in this
epiphanic passage. So much is evident in the already potentially problematic imagery of the golden cup and in the con-
ditionality of the statement: "*If* such unarranged but unerring
encounters gave the measure of the degree in which people
were, in the common phrase, meant for each other, no union
in the world had ever been more sweetened with rightness"
(emphasis added). The lovers nevertheless go a long way toward demonstrating what James called "the great relation between men and women." In retreating from "any but the most
guarded treatment of the great relation between men and
women," James said the novel gave "conspicuous sign that

whatever the prose picture of life was prepared to take upon itself, it was not prepared to take upon itself not to be superficial."[28] The phrase "the great relation" has occasioned snickering at James and irritation at his inferred need to euphemize and idealize sexuality. Actually, however, the phrase aptly suggests the seriousness and exhilaration which the sexual relation at its largest can encompass. For James, sexuality was ultimately a blank whose value was determined by the integers in play.[29] In *The Golden Bowl,* "the great relation" with Charlotte and Amerigo is very great indeed. In the novel's last scene, that greatness is greater still. By making Maggie capable not only of compositional accountability but of the nuances of collaboration in that final intimate moment with Amerigo, James further helps to secure a measure of acceptance for her displacement of Charlotte.

The scene brings together and recharges what has been most controversial in the novel: the ethics of acts of absolute possession, the convergence of authorial and character values and their perhaps inevitable collision, and the yearning for collaborative experience. With Maggie and Amerigo alone at last after the other couple's departure, this is the way the novel ends:

> "Isn't [Charlotte] too splendid?" [Maggie] said, offering it to explain and to finish.
>
> "Oh splendid!" With which [Amerigo] came over to her.
>
> "That's our help, you see," she added—to point further her moral.
>
> It kept him before her therefore, taking in—or trying to—what she so wonderfully gave. He tried, too clearly, to please her—to meet her in her own way; but with the result only that, close to her, her face kept before him, his hands holding her shoulders, his whole act enclosing her, he presently echoed: " 'See'? I see nothing but *you.*" And the truth of it had with this force after a moment so strangely lighted his eyes that as

for pity and dread of them she buried her own in his breast.

(24:368–69)

In the repetitions of the words "splendid" and "see," Maggie and Amerigo seem to advance, as Amerigo and Charlotte did earlier, by "echo[ing]" back to each other their words. But Yeazell suggests that "Reunited though they finally are, Prince and Princess do not speak the same language, nor see in the drama they have enacted the same 'moral,' "[30] and Amerigo's repetition of " 'see' " does perhaps show him "trying [to take] what [Maggie] so wonderfully gave," but not quite succeeding: " ' "See"? I see nothing but *you.*' " On the one hand this limitation of vision evokes the romantic cliché "having eyes for no one but you." It suggests a traditional epiphany in which what is looked at looms so large by virtue of its sudden accession of meaning that it completely fills the vision of the watcher. But such a vow of love also implies a suffocating restriction of real and metaphoric sight. Maggie thus responds with Aristotelian "pity" and "dread," as at the sight of a tragedy, various critics have noted, and we cannot know whether these emotions are ever purged.

The couple's positions in the scene recall their separateness in an earlier scene when, although Maggie at Fawns imagined Amerigo pacing and smoking endless numbers of cigarettes in London, her act of empathic imagining could not fully heal their breach: "*She blinded her eyes* from the full glare of seeing that his idea could only be to wait, whatever might come, at her side. It was to *her buried face* that she thus for a long time felt him draw nearest" (24:295, emphasis added). In the final scene, when they embrace, Maggie again finds herself unable to meet his eyes, and self-blindingly "burie[s] her own in his breast," once more breaking the circuit of their connection. Their embrace, with its willed blindness and questionable harmony, compares unfavorably with the embrace at the end of volume 1 between Fanny and the Colonel who, how-

177

ever comically they may be "face to face" (23:378), yet still
are so.

Amerigo has surrendered to Maggie's fiction of their life;
he has agreed, tacitly, to invent no more independent fictions,
but to live with her in hers, one version, arguably, of what it
means to be married. Very likely it was a similar picture of
married life that James had in mind when he wrote to Grace
Norton, "I am unlikely ever to marry. . . . One's attitude toward marriage is a part—the most characteristic part, doubtless—of one's general attitude toward life. . . . If I were to
marry . . . I should pretend to think just a little better of life
than I really do."[31] We may speculate that James meant he
had difficulty envisioning an intimate relationship that could
sufficiently free itself of the melodramatic polarities of authority and submission, tyranny and renunciation, to make
collaboratively created and mutually satisfying fictions a re-
alizable possibility.

In writing about *Maisie,* James proposed: "No themes are
so human as those that reflect for us, out of the confusion of
life, the close connexion of bliss and bale, of the things that
help with the things that hurt, so dangling before us for ever
that bright hard medal, of so strange an alloy, one face of
which is somebody's right and ease and the other somebody's
pain and wrong" (*Prefaces,* p. 143). The passage promises to
lift itself out of melodrama when it refers to "the confusion
of life," the "connexion of bliss and bale," but the polarized
image of the medal or coin seems to enforce a dualistic vision:
bliss *or* bale, help *or* hurt, right *or* wrong, ease *or* pain.

Nevertheless, while Maggie and Amerigo's final embrace
appears to perpetuate the dualism of mastery and submission,
it also points toward a fusion of possession and surrender so
complex that the distinction between these motives seems almost to disappear. Point of view in the paragraph, even at
times within a single sentence, shifts and merges. When James
writes "He tried, too clearly, to please her—to meet her in

her own way; but with the result only that, close to her, her face kept before him . . . ," we seem to be in Amerigo's consciousness with the exaggerated awareness of the position of Maggie's face, but not when we "too clearly" see, presumably from Maggie's perspective, that he is trying to please. The sentence goes on to convey Amerigo's sense of power in the scene while his words imply a confession of powerlessness— ". . . his hands on her shoulders, his whole act enclosing her, he presently echoed: " ' "See"? I see nothing but *you.*' " The point of view then relocates itself in Maggie's consciousness: "And the truth of it had with this force after a moment so strangely lighted his eyes that as for pity and dread of them she buried her own in his breast." When Amerigo appears to yield to her vision of their fiction by seeing nothing but her, she finds herself possessed—"his whole act enclosing her"— and subdued, overcome by "pity" and "dread."

That James did not fully and consistently escape the drama of dualisms imaged by the medallion does not diminish the importance of his having worked toward that end. Even today, the possibilities of collaboratively imagined and used power are new, and exist, if at all, only in shadowy outline. James anticipated these possibilities of intimacy so movingly, however, that perhaps his value for us now lies most salutarily in that premonitory achievement.

Notes

PREFACE

1. Sallie Sears, *The Negative Imagination: Form and Perspective in the Novels of Henry James* (Ithaca: Cornell University Press, 1968), p. 146.

1 INTRODUCTION: HOUSES OF FICTION

1. Sigmund Freud, "Repression" (1915), in *The Standard Edition of The Complete Psychological Works of Sigmund Freud*, trans. and ed. James Strachey et al., vol. 14, *On the History of the Psycho-Analytic Movement; Papers on Metapsychology; and Other Works* (London: Hogarth Press, 1957), p. 150.

2. Georges Poulet, "Henry James," in *The Metamorphoses of the Circle*, trans. Carley Dawson and Elliot Coleman (Baltimore: Johns Hopkins University Press, 1966), p. 310.

3. Ruth Bernard Yeazell, *Language and Knowledge in the Late Novels of Henry James* (Chicago: University of Chicago Press, 1976), p. 86.

4. Tony Tanner, *The Reign of Wonder: Naivety and Reality in American Literature* (Cambridge: Cambridge University Press, 1965), p. 318.

5. Henry James, *The Letters of Henry James*, ed. Percy Lubbock, vol. 2 (New York: Scribner's, 1920), p. 490.

6. R. W. Stallman, *The Houses that James Built and Other Literary Essays* (East Lansing: Michigan State University Press, 1961), p. 7.

7. J. A. Ward begins *The Search for Form: Studies in the Structure of James's Fiction* (Chapel Hill: University of North Carolina Press, 1967) by discussing James's Romantic concern with organic growth and in-

completeness, and his Neoclassical preference for structure, symmetry, and form. He makes these distinctions serve primarily as a steppingstone to a theory of Jamesian composition he calls "organic architecture" (p. 10), but connects the two imaginative systems without fully pursuing the difficulties posed for James by each.

8. Henry James, *The Question of Our Speech, The Lesson of Balzac* (Boston: Houghton, Mifflin, 1905), pp. 100, 98. Cited hereafter as *Question of Our Speech*.

9. Ezra Pound, "Henry James," in *Literary Essays of Ezra Pound*, ed. T. S. Eliot (1918; reprint, New York: New Directions, 1954), pp. 296, 296 n. 2.

10. Nicola Bradbury, *Henry James: The Later Novels* (Oxford: Clarendon Press, 1979), pp. 3–4, also suggests that there may be a teleological shape to James's opus.

11. Leslie A. Fiedler, *Love and Death in the American Novel* (1960; reprint, Cleveland: World, Meridian, 1962), p. 338.

12. Quentin Anderson, *"The Golden Bowl* as a Cultural Artifact," in *The Imperial Self: An Essay in American Literary and Cultural History* (New York: Knopf, 1971), pp. 161–200.

13. Dorothea Krook, *The Ordeal of Consciousness in Henry James* (Cambridge: Cambridge University Press, 1962).

14. Daniel J. Schneider, *The Crystal Cage: Adventures of the Imagination in the Fiction of Henry James* (Lawrence: Regents Press of Kansas, 1978).

15. Laurence B. Holland, *The Expense of Vision: Essays on the Craft of Henry James* (Princeton: Princeton University Press, 1964), p. 281.

16. Leo Bersani, "The Jamesian Lie," *Partisan Review* 36 (1969): 58.

17. Ibid., pp. 54–55.

18. Saul Rosenzweig, "The Ghost of Henry James," in *Art and Psychoanalysis*, ed. William Phillips (1957; reprint, Cleveland: World, Meridian, 1963), p. 110.

19. Naomi Lebowitz, *The Imagination of Loving: Henry James's Legacy to the Novel* (Detroit: Wayne State University Press, 1965).

20. Yeazell, *Language and Knowledge*, pp. 64–99.

21. See Sergio Perosa, *Henry James and the Experimental Novel* (Charlottesville: University Press of Virginia, 1978), pp. 107–30.

22. Strother B. Purdy, *The Hole in the Fabric: Science, Contemporary Literature, and Henry James* (Pittsburgh: University of Pittsburgh Press, 1977), p. 176.

23. Judith Fryer, *The Faces of Eve: Women in the Nineteenth Century American Novel* (New York: Oxford University Press, 1976), p. 23.

24. Nan Bauer Maglin, "Fictional Feminists in *The Bostonians* and *The Odd Women*," in *Images of Women in Fiction: Feminist Perspectives*, ed. Susan

Koppelman Cornillon (Bowling Green, Ohio: Bowling Green University Popular Press, 1972), pp. 219, 224, 223. See also Wendy Martin, "Seduced and Abandoned in the New World: The Image of Woman in American Fiction," in *Woman in Sexist Society: Studies in Power and Powerlessness,* eds. Vivian Gornick and Barbara K. Moran (New York: Basic Books, New American Library, 1971), pp. 329–46.

25. Judith Fetterley, *The Resisting Reader: A Feminist Approach to American Fiction* (Bloomington: Indiana University Press, 1978), pp. 151, 152.

2 THE MELODRAMA OF HELPLESSNESS

1. F. O. Matthiessen, *The James Family* (New York: Knopf, 1947), p. 273.

2. Ruth Bernard Yeazell, ed., *The Death and Letters of Alice James: Selected Correspondence* (Berkeley: University of California Press, 1981), pp. 15–16, 19.

3. The best general discussion of illness in the James family is Howard M. Feinstein's "The Use and Abuse of Illness in the James Family Circle: A View of Neurasthenia as a Social Phenomenon," *Psychohistory Review* 8, nos. 1–2 (Summer-Fall 1979): 6–14. Feinstein points out that Alice James, like Henry junior, was expert at manipulating the "politics of invalidism" (p. 10), using it to convey feelings not considered legitimate in the Victorian family. The invalid could cause the family pain and anxiety by not improving and by bemoaning a long list of complaints, and at the same time avoid the sense of personal responsibility attendant on direct accusation. Thus Alice James "experienced the intrusion of violence into her consciousness as a physical defect, a 'breakdown in her machinery' or 'muscular insanity,' rather than her own emotional response to her plight" (p. 12). Yet the ill person also suffered guilt for the illness whose benefits he or she enjoyed; "illness helped the sufferer do penance" (p. 13). The portrait drawn by Feinstein coincides with the character of negation discussed in my text. That is, illness of this kind allows the sufferer to defy the family without directly rebelling and achieving a state of independent healthiness.

In the same issue of *Psychohistory Review,* which is devoted in its entirety to the James family, James William Anderson discusses Mary James's contribution to the family pattern of invalidism ("In Search of Mary James," pp. 63–70). Anderson suggests that Mrs. James was interested in her children primarily on occasions of physical illness. This reinforced sickness as a method of getting parental attention, and ensured for her the image of an all-caring, all-nursing, all-denying mother. Her letters consist of catalogues of the physical condition of members of the family, and she constantly emphasized fear and offered warnings, even when her children sent her good news.

4. Sigmund Freud, "Negation" (1925), in Strachey et al., vol. 19, *The Ego and the Id and Other Works* (1961), pp. 235–36.

5. Quoted from the original edition of *The American*, which is most readily available in the Norton Critical Edition: Henry James, *The American*, ed. James W. Tuttleton (New York: Norton, 1978), p. 276. Subsequent quotations from this edition are cited in the text as *American*, orig. ed.

6. Of course there is probably significance in James's need to present Newman as a figure of renunciation notwithstanding. James spares Newman and himself the ultimate test of Newman's difference from other renouncing protagonists: he does not explore whether Newman would still renounce the revenge if by executing it he could reverse the loss of Claire.

7. Richard Poirier, *The Comic Sense of Henry James: A Study of the Early Novels* (New York: Oxford University Press, 1960), p. 65. The book is based on the distinction in James between "fixed" and "free" characters.

8. James W. Gargano, "*Washington Square:* A Study in the Growth of an Inner Self," *Studies in Short Fiction* 13 (1976): 355, 357.

9. Poirier, *Comic Sense*, p. 169.

10. Darshan Singh Maini, "*Washington Square:* A Centennial Essay," *Henry James Review* 1 (1979–1980): 91.

11. Millicent Bell, "Style as Subject: *Washington Square*," *Sewanee Review* 83 (1975): 19.

12. Gargano, "Study," p. 359.

13. Bell, "Style as Subject," p. 19.

14. Ibid., pp. 37, 19, 29.

15. Maini, "Centennial Essay," pp. 96, 97.

16. William Veeder, *Henry James—The Lessons of the Master: Popular Fiction and Personal Style in the Nineteenth Century* (Chicago: University of Chicago Press, 1975), p. 204. Veeder offers further attention to the stylistic means James employs to render the limitedness of Catherine's final gestures, and a fine analysis of the way in which James uses her thoughts and gestures, as well as Sloper's, to challenge the Victorian age's complacency about the genteel standard and his own tendencies to "sound" genteel.

17. Among them, though each is shown as impossible or inadequate for Isabel in one way or another, are life with Caspar Goodwood; life as an independent career woman, in the style of Henrietta Stackpole; and life alone, in the style of Mrs. Touchett. Nina Baym, "Revision and Thematic Change in *The Portrait of a Lady*," *Modern Fiction Studies* 22

(1976–1977): 183–200, shows that James intended Henrietta's example to be taken much more seriously in the original edition: "Henrietta exemplifies a realized independence; she suggests what the 'new woman' has and what she lacks, what she gains and what she sacrifices. . . . She is not merely a *ficelle* in 1881" (p. 193). Baym also notes that, as early as the 1830s, respectable people (including Henry James, Sr.) were associated with the debate over divorce (p. 199).

18. Oscar Cargill, *The Novels of Henry James* (New York: Macmillan, 1961), p. 106.

19. Baym, "Revision," pp. 195 n. 7, 200.

20. Poirier, *Comic Sense*, p. 246. Poirier also views Osmond as "a mock version of the transcendentalist" (p. 219), and "everyone in the novel, except Warburton . . . [as] a self-made man, a version of Emerson's self-subsistent man" (p. 224). One of the parodied transcendental qualities that deserves further study is what James sees as the boredom that results from doing nothing. This boredom is especially in evidence in the novel's opening scene, but it appears throughout. Ralph and both elder Touchetts, Madame Merle, and most of all Osmond, as Madame Merle herself points out in complaining to Isabel of the similarities between her former lover and Ralph (3:280–81), all have nothing to *do* in life, but are occupied solely with being.

The passage from "The Transcendentalist" to which Poirier refers can be found in Emerson, *Nature*, p. 204.

21. Holland, *Expense of Vision*, p. 15.

22. Holland makes a point of the similarity between Osmond's activities and James's own (ibid., pp. 35, 42, 47), but he does not explain what one is to think of Osmond as a stand-in for James, nor how Osmond's sinister quality bears on James's way of regarding himself as an author.

23. William H. Gass, "The High Brutality of Good Intentions," in his collection *Fiction and the Figures of Life* (New York: Knopf, 1970), believes that "There is in Isabel herself a certain willingness to be employed, a desire to be taken up. . . . She will make a great portrait. She knows it," and that "Ralph and Osmond represent two types of the artist" (p. 186), one self-effacing and the other appropriative. He suggests that although "The differences between . . . [them] are vast . . . they are also thin" (p. 188). I prefer to emphasize the differences in James's ideas about authorship represented by Ralph and Osmond in order to explore the two kinds of parental authority basic to independent fiction-making in James.

24. See, for example, Jacques Barzun's 1943 essay "Henry James, Melodramatist," reprinted in *The Question of Henry James: A Collection of Critical Essays,* ed. F. W. Dupee (London: Wingate, 1947), pp. 261–73;

Marius Bewley, *The Complex Fate: Hawthorne, Henry James and Some Other American Writers* (1952; reprint, New York: Gordion, 1967); Leo B. Levy, *Versions of Melodrama: A Study of the Fiction and Drama of Henry James, 1865–1897* (Berkeley: University of California Press, 1957). See also Peter Brooks's commanding study *The Melodramatic Imagination: Balzac, Henry James, Melodrama, and the Mode of Excess* (New Haven: Yale University Press, 1976). Brooks wishes to recover melodrama from its consignment to the rank of secondary genres and effects and he argues, accordingly, that James admires his principal characters' engulfment in melodrama. Brooks focuses on what might be called the melodrama of consciousness, the victimization of being a James narrative center, but locates the source of that victimization in the character's suffering and loss as these are the sign of a transcendent spiritual goodness at the mercy of a manichean world.

25. Poirier, *Comic Sense,* pp. 46, 45.

26. Manfred Mackenzie, "Ironic Melodrama in *The Portrait of a Lady,*" in *Twentieth Century Interpretations of "The Portrait of a Lady,"* ed. Peter Buitenhuis (Englewood Cliffs, N.J.: Prentice-Hall, 1968), pp. 86–87, 92. Mackenzie contends that "Isabel creates, to a large extent anyway, the melodrama of *The Portrait of a Lady.* . . . It is her feeling that makes Osmond remind us of the type from which he derives, the fortune-hunter of melodrama. . . . Her melodramatic imagination absorbs the potentially sensational content of James's plot, with the result that the novel is, yet is not, melodramatic" (p. 89). It is Isabel's choosing to have a melodrama when she might choose otherwise that makes Mackenzie call the melodrama "ironic."

27. See Anthony J. Mazzella, "The New Isabel," in the Norton Critical Edition of *The Portrait of a Lady,* ed. Robert D. Bamberg (New York: Norton, 1975), pp. 597–619, for a detailed discussion of the way in which James's revisions "contribute to the sexual ambience of the 1908 version" (p. 606), most particularly in the characterization of Casper Goodwood. Mazzella concludes: "James suggests that, at heart, what Isabel fears is a loss through the erotic of a special freedom—the freedom of the mind to function unimpeded" (p. 610).

28. John Carlos Rowe, *Henry Adams and Henry James: The Emergence of a Modern Consciousness* (Ithaca: Cornell University Press, 1976), pp. 33, 36.

29. Linda Ray Pratt, "The Abuse of Eve by the New World Adam," in *Images,* ed. Cornillon, p. 168.

30. In *A Feast of Words: The Triumph of Edith Wharton* (New York: Oxford University Press, 1977), Cynthia Griffin Woolf discusses the tendency of newly monied nineteenth-century American society to value

its women as decorative objects, objects of aesthetic contemplation, in psychological and social relation to whom the men assumed the role of collectors (pp. 115, 117).

31. Michael Routh compares this scene of Isabel's appearance framed in a doorway inside of Osmond's house with the moment of Isabel's arrival at Gardencourt when she stands at the threshold of a doorway that leads outside, to the garden. In "Isabel Archer's Double Exposure: A Repeated Scene in *The Portrait of a Lady*," *Henry James Review* 1 (1979– 1980), Routh suggests that the contrast between the outdoor and indoor setting of the two framings adumbrates Isabel's ultimate "entrapment by Osmond" (p. 262). In a similar vein, Juliet McMaster concludes, in "The Portrait of Isabel Archer," *American Literature* 45 (1973–1974): 50–66, that Isabel becomes an object in Osmond's art collection.

3 AMBASSADORIAL CONSCIOUSNESS

1. Quentin Anderson, *Imperial Self;* Richard Poirier, *A World Elsewhere: The Place of Style in American Literature* (New York: Oxford University Press, 1966); Tanner, *Reign of Wonder.* For a survey of criticism that links Emerson and James, see George Sebouhian, "Henry James's Transcendental Imagination," *Essays in Literature* 3 (1976): 224, nn. 2, 3.

2. Stephen Donadio, *Nietzsche, Henry James, and the Artistic Will* (New York: Oxford University Press, 1978), p. 12. Donadio stresses James's similarities to Emerson at the expense, I think, of his divergences.

3. Sears, *Negative Imagination,* pp. x–xi.

4. Poirier, *A World Elsewhere,* pp. 56–57.

5. Roy Harvey Pearce, *The Continuity of American Poetry* (Princeton: Princeton University Press, 1961), p. 184. See also his crystallization of these issues as large problems in our culture and our thinking about community: "It is the problem of defining and making a society in which men can remain individuals and at the same time share values, ideas, and beliefs; in which they can realize themselves as at once different and alike, separate and together, simple and en-masse" (p. 290).

6. Jonathan Bishop, *Emerson on the Soul* (Cambridge: Harvard University Press, 1964), p. 152. Emerson's discussion of this topic can be found in Ralph Waldo Emerson, *The Journals and Miscellaneous Notebooks of Ralph Waldo Emerson,* vol. 8, *1841–1843,* eds. William H. Gilman and J. E. Parsons (Cambridge: Harvard University Press, Belknap Press 1970): 10.

7. Ibid., p. 19.

8. Bishop, *Emerson on the Soul,* p. 157.

9. Quentin Anderson, *Imperial Self,* p. 5.

10. Henry James, "Emerson," in his *Partial Portraits* (London and New York: Macmillan, 1888), pp. 17–18.

11. Henry James, *Notes of a Son and Brother* (New York: Scribner's, 1914), p. 179.

12. Leon Edel, *Henry James,* vol. 1, *The Untried Years: 1843–1870* (New York: Lippincott, 1953), pp. 48, 51.

13. T. S. Eliot, "On Henry James: In Memory," reprinted in *Question of Henry James,* ed. Dupee, p. 125.

14. Poulet, "Henry James," p. 315.

15. Robert C. McLean, "The Subjective Adventure of Fleda Vetch," *American Literature* 36 (1964–1965): 12–30.

16. Richard A. Hocks, *Henry James and Pragmatistic Thought: A Study in the Relationship between the Philosophy of William James and the Literary Art of Henry James* (Chapel Hill: University of North Carolina Press, 1974), p. 144.

17. Henry James, *Letters to A. C. Benson and Auguste Monod,* ed. E. F. Benson (London: Mathews and Marrot, 1930; New York: Scribner's, 1930), p. 35.

18. In *Henry James: The Drama of Fulfillment* (London: Oxford University Press, Clarendon Press, 1975), Kenneth Graham suggests that the spoils are an "image for so many sought-after qualities and powers— personal and impersonal, sexual and aesthetic, moral and social" (p. 138), an image for "the full harmonious life" (p. 157). Graham's is a finely poised meditative reading of the book, which has the interesting effect of removing all sense of oddity or perverseness from Fleda's behavior. There is a brief bibliography of *Spoils* criticism on p. 129, n. 2.

19. The tendency in James criticism even today is to insist that the "free spirit" is compromised by any leanings toward materialism. In *Seeing and Being: The Plight of the Participant Observer in Emerson, James, Adams, and Faulkner* (Middletown, Ct.: Wesleyan University Press, 1981), Carolyn Porter offers this kind of interpretation in a sophisticated Marxist context.

20. Gordon O. Taylor, *The Passages of Thought: Psychological Representation in the American Novel, 1870–1900* (New York: Oxford University Press, 1969), p. 82.

21. Henry James, "The Art of Fiction," in his *Partial Portraits,* p. 389.

22. Holland, *Expense of Vision,* p. 242.

23. Emile Charles Lambinet was a member of the Barbizon school, a group of French painters best known by the work of Rousseau, Cour-

bet, Millet, and Corot, whose landscapes were extremely popular in America and sold well in galleries on Boston's Tremont Street. I am indebted for background information of the group to Robert L. Herbert's catalogue of the 1962 Barbizon exhibit at the San Francisco Palace of the Legion of Honor, *Barbizon Revisited* (New York: Clarke, 1962). Herbert pinpoints the paintings of the Barbizon group as "the first contemporary European works to be acquired in significant quantity by Americans" (p. 10).

24. Viola Hopkins Winner, *Henry James and the Visual Arts* (Charlottesville: University Press of Virginia, 1970), p. 78. See also Charles R. Anderson, *Person, Place, and Thing in Henry James's Novels* (Durham: Duke University Press, 1977), pp. 223, 239–77 passim, for a discussion of the probable influence of specific French Impressionist paintings on various scenes in *The Ambassadors*.

25. Poirier, *A World Elsewhere*, pp. 130–31.

26. James identified the "germ" of *The Ambassadors* as a speech ("Live all you can") delivered by William Dean Howells to Jonathan Sturgis in Paris in 1894 when Howells was "called away—back to America, when he had just come—at the end of 10 days by the news of the death—or illness—of his father" (*Notebooks*, p. 226). Strether's situation echoes Howells's in the sense that both of them are pulled back by relationships which are effectively over, but to which they still feel bound. I do not mean to suggest that James is implying that Howells should not have returned; I simply mean that James interestingly worked the circumstances of that return into the novel on a symbolic level.

27. In the same way that the metaphor of ambassadorship continues to govern the work even when it would seem not to be applicable any longer to Strether, the metaphor of big-game hunting continues to govern James's 1903 story "The Beast in the Jungle" even after Marcher's deflating recognition that he is the man "to whom nothing on earth was to have happened" (17:125). The fact that after this epiphany, Marcher still imagines his fate as a "lurking Beast" (17:127) rising for its leap, and himself as an important and courageous big-game hunter, calls into question his very capacity to have an epiphany, a moment of genuine insight beyond the boundaries of his self-absorbed "mean ego."

28. Yeazell, *Language and Knowledge*, p. 69.

29. See, for example, Lisa Appignanesi, *Femininity and the Creative Imagination: A Study of Henry James, Robert Musil and Marcel Proust* (London: Vision, 1973), p. 76; Gabriel Pearson, "The Novel to End All Novels: *The Golden Bowl*," in *The Air of Reality: New Essays on Henry James*,

ed. John Goode (London: Methuen, 1972), p. 321; and H. Peter Stowell, *Literary Impressionism, James, and Chekhov* (Athens: University of Georgia Press, 1980), pp. 171, 184–85, 214, 219, 234–39.

30. Philip Sicker, *Love and the Quest for Identity in the Fiction of Henry James* (Princeton: Princeton University Press, 1980), p. 164. In the wealth of criticism written on Henry James, Sicker's concerns—identity, love, epiphany—in many ways most closely parallel my own. My emphasis, however, falls upon the sense of self-possession that loving another can enhance, and the way that self-possession makes acts of self-transcendence possible and credible.

In his moving inquiry *The Characters of Love: A Study in the Literature of Personality* (New York: Basic Books, 1960), John Bayley offers a definition of love that is operative in James's world: "That author . . . is best on love who best loves his own creations. . . . What I understand by an author's love for his characters is a delight in their independent existence *as other people,* an attitude towards them which is analogous to our feelings towards those we love in life" (pp. 7–8). This is "the difference between the loved person as an extension of . . . [the perceiver's] consciousness and as a separate" entity (p. 34). Though beautifully exact as a description of the way the self acknowledges the other *as* other in love, this does not do justice to the *reciprocity* of insight created by two people loving each other when, for each, the self as self is profoundly better known.

31. Tanner, p. 318. Other critics who view the novella as a story of the self-sacrificial artist include E. Duncan Aswell, "James's *In the Cage:* The Telegraphist as Artist," *Texas Studies in Language and Literature* 8 (1966–1967): 375–84; and Muriel G. Shine, *The Fictional Children of Henry James* (Chapel Hill: University of North Carolina Press, 1969), pp. 141–45.

32. L. C. Knights, "Henry James and the Trapped Spectator," in his *Explorations: Essays in Criticism, Mainly on the Literature of the Seventeeth Century* (London: Chatto & Windus, 1946), pp. 165, 162; Henry James, *In the Cage & Other Tales,* ed. Morton Dauwen Zabel (1958; reprint, New York: Norton, 1969), p. 12.

33. Jean Frantz Blackall, "James's *In the Cage:* An Approach through the Figurative Language," *University of Toronto Quarterly* 31 (1961–1962): 177.

34. James, *In the Cage & Other Tales,* p. 11.

35. Charles Thomas Samuels, *The Ambiguity of Henry James* (Urbana: University of Illinois Press, 1971), p. 152.

36. Henry James, "Matilde Serao," in *Notes on Novelists with Some Other Notes* (New York: Scribner's, 1914), pp. 299–300.

4 "IMAGINATION IN *PREDOMINANCE*"

1. Bersani, "Jamesian Lie," p. 53.

2. Wayne C. Booth, in *The Rhetoric of Fiction* (Chicago: University of Chicago Press, 1961), argues that James mistakenly sacrifices Maisie's "poignancy" to irony when he changes her from a melodramatic, "helpless victim into a triumphant 'central intelligence' " (p. 48). But James makes Maisie most affecting when she is least a victim, least melodramatically caught in her helplessness, which is toward the end of the novel, when she not only triumphs as a "central intelligence," but brings consciousness to bear on the world.

3. F. R. Leavis, *"What Maisie Knew:* A Disagreement," reprinted in Bewley, *Complex Fate,* p. 130.

4. Harris W. Wilson, "What *Did* Maisie Know?" *College English* 17 (1955–1956): 281.

5. Edward Wasiolek, "Maisie: Pure or Corrupt?" *College English* 22 (1960–1961): 167–72.

6. Shine, *Fictional Children,* p. 118.

7. Bewley, *Complex Fate,* p. 141. Bewley insists upon the air of "horror" and "moral evil" (p. 111) in *Maisie,* which he compares to *The Turn of the Screw.* Leavis counters in his "Disagreement" that there is no "evil," only "squalor" (p. 119).

8. See Bradbury, *Later Novels,* pp. 18, 21, 175, 179 for another discussion of the constructive uses of silence in both *Maisie* and *The Golden Bowl.* Bradbury's subtly modulated reading also touches on the novel's fantasies of violence, which I shall be exploring further, and the respect for others *as other*—the ability to be both inside and outside of her own experience—which makes Maggie "dependable" (p. 161) as a registering consciousness of the scene. Bradbury also emphasizes Maggie's limitations in this respect, however. See as well Stowell's particularly effective discussion of "indirect language" in his *Literary Impressionism,* pp. 230–34.

9. For another way of discussing the reconciliation of dualisms in the novel, and a brief survey of criticism on the novel as "a synthesis of the major thematic oppositions of his earlier work," see a study of spiral form in James by Daniel Mark Fogel: *Henry James and the Structure of the Romantic Imagination* (Baton Rouge: Louisiana State University Press, 1981), p. 85.

10. Samuels, *Ambiguity of Henry James,* p. 224. Sicker believes that although Maggie physically separates from Adam, she never really does give him up: "She escapes both the constrictive prison of the ego and the dissolution of self in another by recognizing two distinct centers of

consciousness [Amerigo *and* Adam] through two equal loves" (*Love and the Quest for Identity*, p. 164).

11. Pearson, "Novel to End All Novels," pp. 348, 341–43.

12. Bersani, "Jamesian Lie," pp. 65, 67.

13. Pearson, "Novel to End All Novels," p. 346.

14. Michael T. Gilmore, *The Middle Way: Puritanism and Ideology in American Romantic Fiction* (New Brunswick, N.J.: Rutgers University Press, 1977), pp. 202–3, 207, 206. Gilmore's way of relating the Fall to the novel's metaphysical concerns seems the most fruitful of the specifically religious approaches to be found in criticism of the novel.

15. Porter believes that the intrusion of a reference to money in this last scene illustrates the "reification" or objectification which makes the world of *The Golden Bowl* irredeemably alienated and dualistic (*Seeing and Being*, p. 135). For her, money is always commodifying, and therefore dualizing, and exists at the expense of the "satisfaction of human desires" (pp. 146, 147), while I see it as a metaphor for such satisfactions—for a necessary and desirable, even if risky, entry into a world of material power, which is the only place where dualism even possibly can be healed.

16. Sicker, *Love and the Quest for Identity*, p. 172.

17. Bradbury (*Later Novels*, p. 191) also notes this instance of self-reflexive narrative wit.

18. Yeazell, *Language and Knowledge*, p. 97.

19. Holland, *Expense of Vision*, p. 347.

20. James, *Question of Our Speech*, p. 92.

21. Ibid., p. 99.

22. Poirier, *The Comic Sense*, p. 8.

23. James, *Question of Our Speech*, p. 98.

24. Pearson, "Novel to End All Novels," p. 332.

25. Philip M. Weinstein, *Henry James and the Requirements of the Imagination* (Cambridge: Harvard University Press, 1971), p. 183.

26. I was helped to this application of my thesis by Christof Wegelin's *The Image of Europe in Henry James* (Dallas: Southern Methodist University Press, 1958), pp. 124–26.

27. Stowell calls this phenomenon "spatial time" (*Literary Impressionism*, p. 234).

28. Henry James, "The Future of the Novel," in *The Future of the Novel: Essays on the Art of Fiction*, ed. Leon Edel (New York: Vintage, 1956), p. 39.

29. In the 1902 essay "Gabriele D'Annunzio," included in his collection *Notes on Novelists*, James writes that the sexual passion is "poetically interesting" for representing something: "it finds its extension and con-

summation only in the rest of life. . . . What the participants do with their agitation . . . or even what it does with them, *that* is the stuff of poetry, and it is never really interesting save when something finely contributive in themselves makes it so" (p. 292).

30. Yeazell, *Language and Knowledge*, p. 125.

31. Henry James, *Henry James Letters*, vol. 2, ed. Leon Edel (Cambridge: Harvard University Press, Belknap Press, 1975), p. 314.

Index

Aestheticism, x, 11, 12, 14. *See also* Style, and authentic emotion

Alienation, 146–148, 151, 192 n. 15

Ambassadors, The, 10, 11, 82–108; and ambassadorial consciousness, 6, 72, 82–83, 99, 107; and capacity for change, 86–91; and "Live all you can" speech, 86–88, 98; and parent-child relationships, 6–7, 91–94, 96–97, 100; preface to, 4–5, 70, 102; and sexuality, 83–84, 89, 91–92, 97, 102–103, 106–107; and styles of painting, 89–90; superlatives in, 85–86; and women, 83–84, 91–92

Characters: Maria Gostrey, 83–84, 92–93, 98–99; Chad Newsome, 100–101, 107; Mrs. Newsome, 6–7, 93–97; Sarah Pocock, 96; Lambert Strether, 4–5, 6, 59, 72, 82–108, 165; Madame de Vionnet, 85, 99–108; Waymarsh, 83, 85–86

Ambassadorship (as metaphor), 6, 71–73, 82–83, 99, 108, 109, 121–123

American, The, 22–31, 35, 36–37; and melodrama, 24–25; and negation, 22–23, 29–30; preface to, 28; and renunciation, 22–23, 27, 28–29, 184 n. 6

Characters: Madame de Bellegarde, 27–30; Claire de Cintré, 27–31, 35, 36–37; Christopher Newman, 23–27, 30, 36–37

Anderson, Quentin, 11, 64, 67

Androgyny, 119–120

Anger: in *The American,* 23–26, 29; in *The Golden Bowl,* 140; in *The Portrait of a Lady,* 49–51; in *Washington Square,* 32, 36; in *What Maisie Knew,* 122

Emerson, Ralph Waldo (Emersonianism), 63–70, 79, 82–83,
104, 106; in *The Portrait of a
Lady*, 39, 40, 41, 55–57, 58–
60, 185 n. 20; and transcendent self, 63–67, 69, 71, 73–74,
80–81, 102, 103–104. *See also*
Eyeball, transparent
Emotion, expression of. *See* Style,
and authentic emotion
Epiphanies, 103–105, 148, 149,
175, 177, 189 n. 27, 190 n. 30.
See also Double epiphanies
Escape (release), 108–120, 125–
126, 130–131, 135–136, 143–
145
European influence, 105–106
Eyeball, transparent (visionary),
63–64, 65–66, 69, 72, 80–81,
136, 167

Fall metaphor, 55–56, 147–148,
192 n. 14
Feinstein, Howard M., 183 n. 3
Feminism, 15–17, 40–41, 68,
119–120, 184 n. 17. *See also*
Women
Fetterley, Judith, 16
Fiedler, Leslie, 11
Financial metaphor. *See* Com-
mercial metaphors
Fogel, Daniel Mark, 191 n. 9
"Free spirit," 69–70, 188 n. 19
French Impressionism, 89–90
Freud, Sigmund, 2, 7, 22, 35, 76,
147
Fryer, Judith, 15

"Gabriele D'Annunzio," 192 n. 29
Garden motif. *See* Soil motif
Gargano, James W., 32

Gass, William H., 185 n. 23
Genteel tradition, 17, 39, 80–81,
114, 184 n. 16
Germ motif. *See* Soil motif
Gilmore, Michael T., 147
Golden Bowl, The, 3–4, 11, 136–
179; and authorship and revision, 136–137, 139, 153–159,
162, 164–169; fantasies of violence in, 139–140, 191 n. 8;
and moral sense, 159–161,
162–164; and parent-child relationship, 137–138, 143–145,
152–153; preface to, 7, 154–
155; and self, 136, 138–139,
147–148, 167–169; and sexuality, 138–139, 145–148, 174–
176; silence and speech in,
138–141, 157, 167, 191 n. 8
Characters: Prince Amerigo,
54, 158–160, 163, 173–179;
Fanny and Bob Assingham,
141–143, 155–158, 177–178;
Bloomsbury merchant, 153–
155, 158–159, 160–161, 162–
164; Charlotte Stant, 160–161,
163, 170–171, 173–176; Adam
Verver, 171–173; Maggie
Verver, 10, 59, 60, 74, 82,
136–150, 164–173, 176–
179
Graham, Kenneth, 188 n. 18

Hawthorne, Nathaniel, 105, 166
Helplessness, 21; and sex, 52–55.
See also Dependence
Hocks, Richard A., 73
Holland, Laurence, 1, 12, 41–42,
88, 159, 185 n. 22
House of fiction, 7–8, 9, 10, 31,
37, 43, 143, 166, 167, 173; in

197

Mysticism, 63. *See also* Double epiphanies; Epiphanies; Self, transcendent

Negation, 20–22, 121–122, 166, 183 n. 3; in *The Ambassadors,* 99; in *The American,* 22–23, 29–30; and Freud, 22, 35; in *The Golden Bowl,* 138–139; and negative space, 2; in *The Portrait of a Lady,* 48, 60–61; in *Washington Square,* 35
Norton, Grace, 178
Notebooks, The, 79–80, 189 n. 26

Oedipal drama, 37, 52; in *The Golden Bowl,* 136, 137–138, 143–145, 152–153, 166; in *What Maisie Knew,* 125–126, 129–131. *See also* Parent-child relationships

Paradise. *See* Eden metaphor
Paradise Lost, 56–57, 87

Parent-child relationships, 6–8; in *The Ambassadors,* 6–7, 91–94, 96–97, 100; in *The American,* 23, 27–30, 35; in *The Golden Bowl,* 137–138, 143–145, 152–153; and the house of fiction, 7, 31, 37, 121, 124, 143; in James family, 13, 18–21, 68, 183 n. 3; in "The Lesson of the Master," 5–6; in *The Portrait of a Lady,* 46–48, 185 n. 23; in *Washington Square,* 20, 31–39; in *What Maisie Knew,* 121–132
Payment, metaphor of, ix, 5, 149–150, 155, 157–159, 161–

162, 164–165, 166–167. *See also* Commercial metaphors
Pearce, Roy Harvey, 66
Pearson, Gabriel, 145–146, 147, 169
Perosa, Sergio, 182 n. 21
Poirier, Richard, 30, 32, 64, 97, 166; on *The Portrait of a Lady,* 41, 46–47
Porter, Carolyn, 187 n. 19, 192 n. 15
Portrait (painting), 61, 171–172, 185 n. 23, 187 n. 31
Portrait of a Lady, The, 39–62; and dependency and freedom, 41–46, 48–49, 52–55, 60–61; and imagination, 39–40, 42; and inability to feel emotion, 49–52; and money, 42–46; preface to, 7, 8–9, 133, 154; and sexuality, 45–46, 53–55; and women, 40–41, 43–44, 47–49, 54–55, 61
  Characters: Isabel Archer, 40–62, 165–166; Caspar Goodwood, 52–58, 186 n. 27; Madame Merle, 48, 50–52, 59; Gilbert Osmond, 41–53 passim, 59–62; Pansy Osmond, 47–49; Henrietta Stackpole, 44, 184 n. 17; Lydia Touchett, 184 n. 17; Ralph Touchett, 42, 43–44, 62
Possession, 55, 80–81; acts of, 168, 176. *See also* Authorship; Commercial metaphors
Poulet, Georges, 2–3, 68, 71
Pound, Ezra, 9, 64
Pratt, Linda Ray, 60–61
Prefaces, 12–13, 173; *The Ambassadors,* 4–5, 70, 102; *The Ameri-*

iations which conclude
novels have for a long
ocus of critical contro-
's value and relevance
readers.   Carren
James views renun-
not only of an em-
ne capable of reg-
l points of view of
iated" self, a self
s "center" to the
nce created by
ns.

merican literature
erson's image of the
t eyeball, this para-
ood defines what it
aracter of conscious-
lies at the heart of his
ard these figures. In
alled the melodrama of
James shows his charac-
ousness to be victims of ty-
overpowering parent-author
velling in parental, often
ouses of fiction," the charac-
sciousness are unable to claim
selves such forbidden "spoils"
ial experience as love and sex-
ames viewed his sacrificial pro-
s as, in an important sense,
thors, failed imaginers of their
erience. They possess only what
lled "imagination galore," not
comprehensive "imagination
ance," imagination "in *supreme*
of a case or of a career." The
ting imagination is a mediat-
: it empowers consciousness
fillment in the world.
reading adjusts the prevailing
f James as an aesthete, a writer
lieved that the highest art re-
the renunciation of materially
ng forms of power and being. It
James searching for a way simul-
ly to transcend the self and to
he self at its desiring center.